MORE THAN A PROPHET

KEY LESSONS IN RAISING FORERUNNERS
FROM THE LIFE OF JOHN THE BAPTIST

ROGER LEE

Sarasota House of Prayer
Publishing

MORE THEN A PROPHET
Key Lessons in Raising Forerunners from the Life of John the Baptist
Copyright ©2018 by Roger Lee
Published in the United States of America

Printed in the United States of America
ISBN-13:978-1719196024
ISBN-10:1719196028

Scripture Quotations taken from the "Scripture quotations taken from the New American Standard Bible® (NASB), Copyright © 1960, 1962, 1963, 1968, 1971, 1972, 1973, 1975, 1977, 1995 by The Lockman Foundation
Used by permission. www.Lockman.org"

Published by Sarasota House of Prayer Publishing
Sarasota House of Prayer
1872 18th St.
Sarasota, FL 34234

Cover design by Ethan Byerly

Sarasota House of Prayer
www.sarasotahop.com

DEDICATION

This book is dedicated to my beloved wife,
Jennifer.

Thank you for your unending love and support.
God sent you to me so that we can skip down the
narrow road together! You are my best friend and
ever so grateful for you and your life in God!
I love you forever and into eternity.

To our ten wonderful children:
Josiah, Rael, Daniel, Caleb, Micah
Ariel, Zion, Bethany, Moriah and Zoe!

You bring so much joy and laughter to our lives.
God has made you each so unique and special. I
am so proud of each of you. I love you all!

MORE THAN A PROPHET
KEY LESSONS IN RAISING FORERUNNERS
FROM THE LIFE OF JOHN THE BAPTIST

ACKNOWLEDGEMENTS

Jim and Sandra Good
Thank you for your faithful friendship.
It means more to me than you will know.

My Mom and Dad
Thank you for your constant support and love.
I love you both!

My family and friends
You have encouraged me through the years and am
grateful for each of your influence in my life.

To the staff at the Sarasota House of Prayer
You guys are the best. Keep the fire burning!
Let's go change the world!

Dannie Phillips and Jane Casey
All of your help in getting this book published.

Ethan Byerly
Cover design and graphic work.

MORE THAN A
PROPHET

KEY LESSONS IN RAISING FORERUNNERS
FROM THE LIFE OF JOHN THE BAPTIST

ROGER LEE

Sarasota House of Prayer
Publishing

PREFACE

A voice is calling, "Clear the way for the LORD in the wilderness; Make smooth in the desert a highway for our God. (Isaiah 40:3)

God is raising up forerunners in our day in the likeness of John the Baptist to be voices in the wilderness. Many are called to this type of lifestyle and message which will be translated through a number of different ways. I believe in this generation the Lord is sovereignly raising up messengers to impact every sphere of society, and is releasing *strategic, innovative ideas* to get the message across. As the forerunner message is proclaimed, multitudes resonate with its core values in their spirits. They become excited as it begins to give verbiage and understanding to why their lives have looked different from their friends. Many have grown up and carried a seemingly different, more intense desire in their hearts for the person of Jesus and His unique purposes for this generation. They feel out of place and don't seem to fit into the status quo of what the Christian landscape is offering. There is a desperate cry that has been lodged deep within their hearts for more! I have found many that are walking through life in this situation but have not understood the call of God on their lives.

There is another important aspect that goes along with identifying the forerunner calling, it is the principles of preparation and training the Lord puts all His servants through. Many with the genuine call to be forerunners in this generation, though they may not have been able to articulate it in this way, have not understood the dealings of God in their lives and over time have been waylaid and sidetracked with disappointment and offense at God. They have not been able to reconcile why they live with this intense desire for more, why some continuously have dreams of the end times and judgments, why they seemingly "know" things and are able to discern people and situations yet nothing seems to materialize in their lives like the way they thought it would, or have been promised by God through prophetic utterances.

- Why have I had this intense desire for the Lord?

- Why do I not fit in with other Christian friends?

- Why do I keep having intense dreams of judgment and the end times?

- Why do people not seem to understand me?

- Why do I "know" things about people and situations?

- Why do I see the hypocrisy of the religious system when everyone seems to be oblivious to it?

- Why is God overlooking me for promotions?

- Why are my gifts and talents being hidden?

- Why do I feel like this wilderness will never end?

Through looking at key life lessons from John the Baptist and sharing parts of my own journey, it is my desire to impart budding forerunners with: understanding and confidence in the call of God over their lives, insight into the process by which God trains and prepares His forerunners, and vision to walk with God in this unique way.

Roger Lee

CHAPTER 1

SKY'S THE LIMIT

God's Unique Training for His Forerunners

Driving up windy Red Bridge road in Kansas City in May, I felt the Lord impressing upon my heart an understanding that "If you go with her (Jennifer, my fellow intern), the sky's the limit." It was an aha moment for me. Here was God's invitation for me to enter His training ground. It wasn't seminary, bible school or anything that I had hoped for or imagined. Instead the Lord had an arduous wilderness season set aside for me - specifically for the next twelve years - that would reveal, expose and train my heart in the grace of God. More than that, He had a desert with desire and intimacy through which He wanted to make Himself known to me!!! Beloved, the Lord has this type of season for every genuine forerunner! He is jealous over our lives to reveal Himself and prepare us; His divinely crafted seminary prepares and tests our hearts so that we would be able to steward the anointing and authority that He will release in the days to come.

I was coming to the end of an internship at Master's Commission, a nine-month residential discipleship program that was part of Metro Christian Fellowship in Kansas City, Missouri, under Mike Bickle; this was my second and last year of the program. I graduated from Master's Commission in 1998 and was now serving as an intern on staff at Metro. I had been dating a woman back in Seattle via long-distance relationship for about three years. After being immersed in a completely different environment at Metro Christian Fellowship we had drifted apart. Towards the end of my internship and as part of the study program, we were going through the book, <u>Finding the Love of Your Life</u>. An assignment was to list the negotiable and non-negotiable traits that we were looking for in a spouse. As I was making my list and reviewing it, subconsciously I was comparing Jennifer, my fellow intern, to my long-distance relationship from Seattle. I suddenly realized that I was in love with Jennifer! Another aha moment! The problem was that everyone at home in Seattle expected me to get married to this woman when I was done with Kansas City; however, as I compared the two, in every respect, Jennifer was so much greater! I was in a major dilemma.

GROWING UP IN SEATTLE

I was restless with thoughts and pressures of what people back home were saying and what was stirring in my heart. I had grown up in Seattle when I received the Lord during my second year at the University of Washington where I was studying to become a family practice physician; I was very active in the youth groups of Korean churches in the Seattle area and on campus. I was being groomed to follow my pastor's example where he was in full-time ministry while his wife worked as a pharmacist to support the family financially. My girlfriend at that time was in a Doctor of Pharmacy program to become a pharmacist to support her family and ministry. Also, many of my friends had gone to Regent Seminary in Vancouver BC (about 3 hours away) to get their Masters of Divinity. There was a definite, well-understood path laid out in the Korean Christian community if you wanted to become a pastor. You first go to seminary to get your degree. As you do, you serve as a youth pastor, paying your dues and rising up the church leadership ladder. While serving as a youth pastor of a local Korean church, there are retreat circuits, especially in the summer, that many would teach and network in to get their names out. Finally, you "graduate" to become a senior pastor or branch off to start your own 2nd -generation English speaking church. Every ethnic culture has their religious pathway, but this was mine. I was looking ahead to the future with the next five years of my life already determined to get into what we called "ministry." But when I saw the path, I felt trapped! To me, the entire system of "climbing the spiritual ladder of ministry" in the Korean culture seemed unbiblical and shrouded with religion. It was less about having a passion for Jesus and how one's callings, anointings, and giftings fit into building the Kingdom of God and more about knowing the right people and doing the right things. This idea, in essence, is how the religious system entraps a culture and chocks out the spiritual life that brings transformation.

Driving up Red Bridge Road on that fateful Sunday afternoon in 1999, I was contemplating all these options. I felt trapped as I was looking at going back home to Seattle. On the one hand, I had someone to marry who would ensure a safe financial future, a pathway for ministry through a good school with many people to support me in the journey, and a home church who was grooming me. On the other hand, there was Jennifer! She was glowing in beauty and godliness! There was such a fresh hunger for God and His purposes that radiated through her that I had never encountered. She had become my best friend and had challenged me on so many issues during our internship together. We would debate, talk for hours, and "fix" all the problems of the Church in the little office that we worked in together. I had unknowingly admired her, and she had captured my heart!

Oh, the Dilemma! What to do? Do I go the safe route back home or do I follow my heart and go with Jennifer? To me, Seattle represented the religious system - secure but lifeless. Jennifer represented the unknown and breaking away from the expectations of people and tradition. In the midst of this, the Lord broke through and spoke to me: "If you go with Jennifer, the sky's the limit." I had little-to-no understanding of what that meant other than God had said "if," meaning I still had the choice to make. I couldn't comprehend what God had in mind for us in the future other than leaving behind what I had known to go after the *rhema* word of God over my life, and it meant that I get to have Jennifer! This was a clear fork in the road with significant consequences. The time had come to decide.

I believe that the Lord is training forerunners in this generation in ways that are unconventional or out of the box to break off the tentacles of tradition and the religious system. He is raising up leaders and forerunners in the new wineskin who can steward the movements of God in the unique dynamics of the End Times and can reach back into the old religious system to pull others out. This strategy has been God's way through history as He raises up deliverers in each generation.

JOHN THE BAPTIST'S HERITAGE

**[5]*In the days of Herod, king of Judea, there was a priest named Zacharias, of the division of Abijah; and he had a wife from the daughters of Aaron, and her name was Elizabeth. [6]They were both righteous in the sight of God, walking blamelessly in all the commandments and requirements of the Lord.*
*(Luke 1:5-6)***

We are introduced to John the Baptist through his parents Zacharias and Elizabeth. John had a rich priestly heritage in his family line. His father Zacharias served as a priest in the kingdom of Israel where he was on a rotation to enter the temple of the Lord and burn incense. The Bible tells us that both Zacharias and Elizabeth were "righteous" in the sight of God and blameless in all the commandments and the requirements of the Lord (Luke 1:6). This means that John was born into a healthy, intact family which we cannot take for granted in our day. More than that, he was raised in the admonition of the Lord and with the values of Yahweh. Zacharias and Elizabeth had a loving marriage which brought stability and life to his family. John grew up in what we would call a "good Christian home" with godly parents who loved the Lord.

John also had a distinct feature in his lineage - his mother Elizabeth was related to Mary the mother of Jesus as a kinsman or a general relative. They were not literal "first cousins" by family line but had some family connection. Mary came from the tribe of Judah and Elizabeth from the tribe of Levi. However, when Elizabeth was six months pregnant with John, Mary came to visit her in her home and stayed three months with her (Luke 1).

THE GREATEST MAN BORN OF A WOMAN

"Truly I say to you, among those born of women there has not arisen anyone greater than John the Baptist! Yet the one who is least in the kingdom of heaven is greater than he. (Matthew 11:11)

John the Baptist had a truly unique and unprecedented ministry, which we will look at in much more depth throughout this book. To whet your appetite and get your mind started, consider this: Jesus called John the "greatest man born of a woman" in Matthew 11:11. He was commenting on John's life and ministry and referencing John against the backdrop of all the great Old Testament men of God, men like Abraham, Moses, Samuel, David, Isaiah, Daniel, Jeremiah, Elijah, etc. Amazingly, looking back through Israel's history, Jesus tells us that there is one man who stood above them all - it was John. What a compliment on John's life and that is an understatement! However, when we take a closer look at John's life, that statement by Jesus is puzzling.

Many came to Him and were saying, "While John performed no sign, yet everything John said about this man was true." (John 10:41)

Compared to some of the great men of Israel's history, John had a very short ministry without the power dimension of miracles through which Moses and Elijah operated. Though John was prepared for thirty years in the wilderness, his ministry only lasted about six months before he was put into prison by Herod. Even more perplexing is that there were no signs or wonders that accompanied John's ministry yet he was able to baptize up to 1.5 million Jews in the wilderness and prepare a generation to receive Jesus as Messiah. This was the strength of John's ministry - anointed preaching that moved a nation in the power and spirit of Elijah!

MORE THAN A PROPHET

"But what did you go out to see? A prophet? Yes, I tell you, and one who is more than a prophet. (Matthew 11:9)

John was a prophet of the Lord! Yes, but more than a prophet! He not only brought a prophetic message to Israel, but he was also called "My Messenger" by Jesus. John was the fulfillment of the one who was spoken of by Isaiah the prophet in Isaiah 40, and the "messenger" prophesied that would come before the Lord in Malachi 3. John was "more than a prophet" in that he was the chosen "messenger" to prepare the way of the Lord for Jesus' first coming. I believe this messenger was made into the message in the wilderness years of his life. He was more than just a prophetic voice for his generation; *he was able to understand and carry the heart of God to become the message itself.* There is a huge distinction between giving a message and becoming the message, and John's life itself was the message to the nation. The Lord is still yet at work calling and preparing holy lives, set apart to become the message of God's heart, to be released into the nations in this generation! The fact that you are moved by John's life and even reading this book tells me that this messenger-type forerunner anointing is resonating in your heart!

"This is the one about whom it is written, 'Behold, I send My Messenger ahead of you, who will prepare your way before you.' (Matthew 11:10)

UNIQUENESS SURROUNDING JOHN'S BIRTH

Zacharias and Elizabeth, though righteous, were old and without children. To her shame in that culture, Elizabeth was barren. They both bore this reproach in their community as the culture blamed individuals who could not have children as having sin in their lives. So when Elizabeth miraculously became pregnant and bore John, it was part of God's vindication. We will look at several unique events that surrounded John's miraculous birth.

There was a supernatural announcement made about John's birth and life. While John's father Zacharias was performing his priestly service in the temple, Gabriel the angel appeared to him and announced John's name and assignment. The angel Gabriel is only mentioned four times in the entire Bible and this is one of them - to give John's name. The fact that Gabriel was sent by God the Father should highlight the importance of John's life to us. Understanding that God provides a forerunner before Christ appears at both His first and second comings further points to John like a neon sign to our generation that we need to understand how God raised up this prototypical forerunner. That is how significant John's forerunner ministry was in God's plans. Gabriel also made Zacharias mute, unable to speak because of his unbelief, so the people knew Zacharias had a supernatural encounter while offering the incense! When Zacharias' mouth was loosed, great fear fell upon the people concerning John's future!

But the angel said to him, "Do not be afraid, Zacharias, for your petition has been heard, and your wife Elizabeth will bear you a son, and you will give him the name John. (Luke 1:13)

[59]And it happened that on the eighth day they came to circumcise the child, and they were going to call him Zacharias, after his father. [60]But his mother answered and said, "No indeed; but he shall be called John." [61]And they said to her, "There is no one among your relatives who is called by that name." (Luke 1:59-61)

The Lord Himself gave John his name and delivered it through Gabriel! John was named by Heaven. This is very significant because nobody else in their family line had this name. Culturally, John would have taken his father's name to honor the family line. However, the Lord spoke to both parents, Zacharias and Elizabeth, that John would take on a name that went against their tradition. Giving the new name of John into the family line is symbolic of what the Lord wanted to do in the identity of His forerunner. I believe it speaks to the breaking away from the traditions of men so that he would be set apart unto the Lord.

"For he will be great in the sight of the Lord; and he will drink no wine or liquor, and he will be filled with the Holy Spirit while yet in his mother's womb.
(Luke 1:15)

*⁴¹When Elizabeth heard Mary's greeting, the baby
leaped in her womb; and Elizabeth was filled with the
Holy Spirit…⁴⁴"For behold, when the sound of your
greeting reached my ears, the baby leaped in my
womb for joy. (Luke 1:41,44)*

Gabriel called forth John's destiny as a Nazarite from the womb, one who is dedicated and separated for the Lord (Numbers 6). This shows that God had consecrated John's entire life as one that is holy unto the Lord, sacred for His purposes. He was even filled with the Holy Spirit while in his mother's womb!

John had every advantage to prosper and succeed in the traditional sense. He was instilled with the foundation of a healthy, godly family and his parents modeled a loving marriage before him. By birth he was of the privileged priestly line thus his calling and future were secure. He was set to "climb the spiritual ladder of ministry," yet John would not follow his culture's religious pathway. The sacred priesthood was passed on through the bloodline and so protected and reserved for the family of Levi. His birth was marked by many supernatural signs and wonders that brought the fear of the Lord upon the region. However, these God-given advantages were not enough to prepare God's chosen forerunner; Instead, he followed the Lord into the wilderness to be trained by Him for his divine assignment. God called me into the wilderness for training, and He has called or is calling you too!

OUR LOVE STORY

As a side note to finish our love story, I asked Jennifer to meet me after our home group the night the Lord spoke to me. We sat together on an old railroad tie in the parking lot of the International House of Prayer (IHOPKC) trailers, which had just opened a couple of weeks prior. I held her hand and began to pour my heart out to her of all that was going on in the past couple of weeks and about going to the nations together to serve the Lord. I was nervous about what she would say… She said YES! And life has never been the same.

KEY UNDERSTANDING

I have found a key concept to understanding God's way of preparing forerunners. Most people believe God is preparing them to make an impact in the current system. *However, I believe that God is preparing forerunners **now** according to the climate in which they will operate in the **future**.* I think future systems will be much different and more difficult, and thus the training now is more demanding. Without understanding this concept, people get discouraged and want to give up because the difficulty of preparation is not commensurate with their lives. However, if we realize that God is preparing us for another time and another context, then it gives us understanding to partner wholeheartedly with God's preparation, and it relieves us of the self-inflicted pressure of success.

A PRAYER FOR BUDDING FORERUNNERS

Dear Heavenly Father,

I pray for the many budding forerunners you are preparing in this very hour whose spirits bear witness to your call but have not understood your ways. Give them a courageous spirit to continue to press into you and to follow the dreams that you have given them. Strengthen their inner man that they would not quit the race but that You, Lord, would mold their hearts to be able to steward the anointing and the weight of the glory that You want to release upon them. I pray especially for those who have been walking through the wilderness, some for many years, that a spirit of might would come upon them in a tangible way.

Father of Glory, raise up anointed and humble messengers to fulfill your redemptive purposes in our generation! Release a spirit of wisdom and revelation even now as they read this book that these would have insight, with understanding, in how you have been preparing them so they can partner with your glorious heart.

In Jesus' glorious name we pray for the keeping of your precious forerunners!

AMEN!

28

CHAPTER 2

BIBLICAL FORERUNNERS

Strategic Forerunners for Transitional Generations

"It is he who will go as a forerunner before Him in the spirit and power of Elijah, to turn the hearts of the fathers back to the children, and the disobedient to the attitude of the righteous, so as to make ready a people prepared for the Lord." (Luke 1:17)

As we read the story of redemption from Genesis to Revelation, we see highlighted moments in God's storyline where He relates to His people in new ways. Though He is the same God, He gave His people Israel the revelation and guidelines of the sacrificial system in the book of Exodus as a new way to relate to Him. After the Father sent His only begotten Son, God related to the redeemed based on the finished work of Christ on the cross. No longer was it acceptable to have a relationship with God through the Old Covenant sacrificial system. Now it was through the new and living way of the offering of the flesh of the Son of God on the cross (Hebrews 10:20).

These are examples in which God's fundamental way of relating to humanity has changed or evolved. These changes in the basis of relationship or when God makes a covenant come about to reveal more of who God is, to give the people of God greater access to Him and for the Lord to administer His plan of redemption further. We call these strategic generations where the fundamental way in which God relates to mankind changes "transitional generations." In these transitional generations, God raises up a strategic forerunner to prepare the people by giving them an understanding of what God is doing. We will look at three primary transitional generations the Bible speaks about starting with the generation of Moses.

THE GENERATION OF MOSES

The Lord heard the oppressed cry of His people in Egypt and prepared a deliver in the wilderness - Moses! By an outstretched arm and with great judgments, God showed Himself as Yahweh and delivered the Israelites from the army of Pharaoh. He brought them through the Red Sea, into the wilderness of Sinai and finally to the foot of the mountain of God! Here, God entered into a marriage covenant with the people of Israel called the Mosaic Covenant (Exodus 19-24). Part of this covenant was the building of the tabernacle of Moses, including the sacrificial system so that God may dwell among them (Ex. 25:8; 29:45-46). This period was a transitional generation in which God raised up Moses as a forerunner to prepare the people of Israel in how to have a relationship with God. Moses led the people of God in his generation primarily through incredible signs and wonders of which the majority of the people witnessed on a regular basis. They observed God's power against the nation of Egypt, walked through the Red Sea as it parted before them, saw the mountain of God ablaze with fire as God came down to give them the 10 commandments, ate the manna daily, followed the fire by night and cloud by day in the wilderness, drank the water from the rock in the desert and so on. There was an awe-inspiring display of power in this generation, which is why Moses was revered. What Moses was not known for, however, was power in his preaching.

Interestingly, when God is strategically preparing His deliverer, the enemy seeks to eliminate the forerunner preemptively. This strike was manifested in the murdering of innocent children as Pharaoh gave the order to kill every son out of fear (Exodus 1:22). This abortion spirit to root out God's forerunner was also prevalent in our next transitional generation - the generation of Jesus.

[35]"This Moses whom they disowned, saying, 'Who made you a ruler and a judge?' is the one whom God sent to be both a ruler and a deliverer with the help of the angel who appeared to him in the thorn bush. [36]"This man led them out, performing wonders and signs in the land of Egypt and in the Red Sea and in the wilderness for forty years. (Acts 7:35-36)

THE GENERATION OF JESUS

In the first century, we have two forerunners who were born roughly six months apart - John the Baptist and Jesus of Nazareth. Jesus was THE FORERUNNER who opened our access to the heavenly temple. We will look closer at Jesus's forerunner ministry later. John, however, was chosen by the Lord as the forerunner to prepare the people of Israel to receive Jesus. In the last chapter, we looked at some of the unique supernatural phenomena that surrounded John's birth. He was sovereignly raised up to prepare the Jews to relate to God in intimacy through the One He sent, namely Jesus, the God who took on our form as a man. John received the revelation of Jesus as the Lamb of God (John 1:29) who takes away the sin of the world. It was through this Lamb of God who, not only fulfilled all the righteous requirements of the Torah but through the shedding of His blood, brought forth eternal salvation along with the gift of the indwelling Holy Spirit. God again changed the way humanity was to relate to Him - now it was through the person of His Son with the more extraordinary privilege of receiving His imputed righteousness and the indwelling Holy Spirit! This way of relating far surpassed the Mosaic covenant and the old sacrificial system.

The Lord sent John the Baptist as His Messenger ahead of Jesus to prepare the people just as He did with Moses. John was anointed with the spirit and power of Elijah (Luke 1:17) as foretold by the angel Gabriel to Zacharias. However, when we look at John's ministry in the first century, the spirit and power of Elijah had a different manifestation than it did with the original Elijah or even Moses. John did not walk in the power dimension of signs and wonders or miracles. The Bible tells us explicitly in John 10:41 that John the Baptist did no signs in his ministry yet his preaching in the wilderness had such an anointing on it that he was able to pierce the dark atmosphere of his generation and prepare a nation! This preaching anointing was filled with the spirit and power of Elijah!

Jesus was a different kind of forerunner than John or Moses. He wasn't just preparing the people for what was to come; instead, He entered into the Holy of Holies of the perfect tabernacle in Heaven (Hebrews 9:11) through the shedding of His blood to make a way for us to follow. In this eternal sense, He blazed a trail as the forerunner who has gone before us so that we can enter into the holiest place in Heaven above both now and for eternity.

> *where Jesus has entered as a forerunner for us,*
> *having become a high priest forever according to the*
> *order of Melchizedek. (Hebrews 6:20)*

THE END-TIME GENERATION

There is more written prophetically about this last end-time generation than any other generation in the Bible! It will culminate with Jesus returning in the clouds to initiate the Day of the Lord, which the Old Testament prophets spoke about often. The Day of the Lord is described as being great, terrible and awesome at the same time. It will be great for the believers who love Jesus and are waiting for His return. It will be immensely terrible for the unbelievers as the Lord releases His judgments against the Antichrist system and removes unrighteousness from the Earth. As the Father transitions the Earth in a single generation for the return of His Beloved Son, the events that will happen, understood through the right grid, will make us stand in awe of the wisdom and power of God! I believe God is preparing end-time forerunners who will operate in the full manifestation of the power and spirit of Elijah. They will move in the power dimensions of Moses **and** Elijah with great signs and wonders as well as the power dimension of John the Baptist with the unique anointing in preaching that moved a nation! We see a preliminary measure of this type of authority in the Book of Acts as the early apostles preached with conviction and ministered in the miraculous but only within the boundaries of Israel. In the last generation, God will raise up forerunners all over the earth who will perform the "greater works than these" (John 14:12) against the background of darkness. This is what we are being prepared for!

WHAT IS A FORERUNNER?

The term "forerunner" is in vogue and made popular in our Christian culture but is actually only used twice in the Bible. It is used first to describe John the Baptist in Luke 1:17, and then of what Jesus accomplished in Hebrews 6:20. However, the idea or principle of the forerunner is evident throughout the Bible. The word "forerunner" means to go forward, to go before, precede or go in advance of another. A forerunner means a person or thing that heralds the coming or development of someone or something else. It is also a sign or warning of something to come. Forerunners are ones that go ahead of the rest, preparing, warning and making a way for the rest of the people to enter. The idea of the forerunner is similar to the principle of first fruits in that they are a first part that represents the whole. Forerunners are part of the Body of Christ and are not more special or elite, but their assignment is different in that they are called to go before to prepare the Body of Christ to enter into what God has offered. Other similar terms that have become popular to represent this idea of the forerunner are pioneers, trailblazers, and more generically, leaders.

THE PURPOSE OF THE FORERUNNER

There are multiple reasons why God raises up a forerunner, but we will focus on three primary purposes. The first reason is that forerunners "go ahead" or go first into areas to establish, clear the way and make a path. They usually initiate, build, begin new ideas, and go into places that are foreign or not always comfortable to the Gospel. The Lord sends them into places to bring about or establish a certain level of the Kingdom of God. A great example of this is the apostle Paul who was sent out from Antioch in Acts 13 to begin bringing the Gospel to the Gentile world. As Paul and Barnabas intentionally brought the Gospel to the Gentiles, it opened the door for others to follow them to minister in these new areas. When forerunners initiate new works, it creates a "bubble" into which other believers can enter into and find their right place in the work of God. Because of this, it takes courage and trust established between the forerunner and the Lord to submit to what God wants in the midst of difficulties and trials as the new work is beginning.

The second purpose for the forerunner is to open the gate so that the rest of the people may enter in! The focus isn't on the forerunner themselves or their ministry; it is rightly on the people of God. God wants the entire body to enter into His promises! This is the correct perspective. Forerunners are not "better" or "more elite" than the group, but their assignment is to go ahead and prepare the way so that the rest of the group can follow the footsteps carved out for them. Many in the charismatic circles are enamored with their perceived call to be a "forerunner" or "pioneer" and focus on how special they are instead of operating from the larger picture that God is using them for the higher purpose of building up the Body of Christ and the nations. He raises up and anoints a forerunner to further His Kingdom administration and to align the Body of Christ with His plans which culminate at the end of the age! Biblical leadership is given to serve for the betterment of others. This is the purpose of raising up forerunners - to help the Body of Christ. It is to prepare a way for others to walk in the purposes of God. We cannot overstate this in our day. Even in the Christian culture we have elevated positions and titles, thinking they are an end to themselves, almost having pop-star or rock star status. However, the Lord is jealous for His glory and is changing the heart posture and mindset of a forerunner generation who is in it for the Lord and His glory alone! *They are willing to forsake the "praise of men" to partner with God.* Their lone cry is "I must have more of God!" John the Baptist said clearly, "He must increase, but I must decrease." (John 3:30). This is the kind of model that King David, the first-century apostles, and others who fulfilled the Lord's purposes have given us to follow. Even Jesus Himself came to serve and not to be served in establishing the way of salvation for mankind.

And David realized that the LORD had established him as king over Israel, and that He had exalted his kingdom for the sake of His people Israel.
(2 Samuel 5:12)

⁹For, I think, God has exhibited us apostles last of all, as men condemned to death; because we have become a spectacle to the world, both to angels and to men. ¹⁰We are fools for Christ's sake, but you are prudent in Christ; we are weak, but you are strong; you are distinguished, but we are without honor. ¹¹To this present hour we are both hungry and thirsty, and are poorly clothed, and are roughly treated, and are homeless; ¹²and we toil, working with our own hands; when we are reviled, we bless; when we are persecuted, we endure; ¹³when we are slandered, we try to conciliate; we have become as the scum of the world, the dregs of all things, even until now. (1 Corinthians 4:9-13)

END TIME FORERUNNERS

Just as in the days of old, the Lord is preparing for another transition. This time it's not just a nation, like what He did with Israel, but the entire planet! God is going to transition the earth from this age to the age to come by the return of Jesus to usher in the Millennial Kingdom. Then Jesus will relate to His people in a different way, a more intimate way in which He will be physically present with a glorified body on the Earth in Jerusalem again. This transition involves many dynamics as God is going to shake everything that can be shaken before the great and terrible Day of the Lord. In preparation for this, the Lord is raising up forerunners to be voices of truth and warning, to give understanding of what is to come and how to navigate through the days ahead. *The fact that forerunners are being prepared and emerging in itself is a sign that God is on the move in our generation.* As the New Testament forerunners and apostles pointed to Jesus and His work on the Cross, I believe the end-time Forerunners will point to Jesus and His glorious return!

I believe one of the most significant areas of impact that end-time forerunners will have is in bringing an understanding to God's judgments. As we draw closer to the second coming of Christ, God will send His wrath upon the Antichrist empire (Revelation 8, 9, 16). These unprecedented and dramatic judgments are to remove the evil off the earth and to bring justice against the most vile oppressor the world has ever seen. God's judgments are not against the Church, but for the sake of the Church, to judge evil and establish righteousness on the earth. When God judges temporal sin, it is an expression of His love to remove evil. However, the severity of God's judgments and the releasing of His wrath are not well understood in our day and have become very unpopular. When the end-time events begin to escalate, and these Biblical judgments are released, many in the Church will not have an understanding and be offended at God. This is where forerunners must step in. They will interpret God's judgments and give interpretation so that the Church will submit to Jesus' leadership and mature in love. The reason God judges the Antichrist is to remove the greatest oppressor and save the oppressed. At the same time, He offers mercy and salvation to those doing the oppressing. This is God's all-encompassing way of showing love and justice on the earth at the same time to all involved.

KEY UNDERSTANDING

Throughout history, there are unique transitional generations in which the way God relates to His people changes. In these dynamic generations, God raises up a forerunner or a company of forerunners to prepare His people by shedding light on what God is doing. This pattern is once again being fulfilled in our generation as God is raising up a company of end-time forerunners to prepare the way for the Lord's return. These end-time forerunners will boldly proclaim the second coming of Christ and make the global Church ready to navigate in victory through the unparalleled difficulties and opportunities that are on the horizon.

A PRAYER FOR FORERUNNERS

Dear Heavenly Father,

Thank you for allowing us to be alive in this transitional generation! We have the privilege of watching Your redemptive history unfolding before our very eyes.

I am asking that You would raise up a new breed of leaders and forerunners to lead the Church in this hour. Release upon these forerunners a spirit of wisdom and revelation to understand what You are doing in the nations. Raise up these end-time forerunners who have the anointing of the sons of Issachar, to know the times and seasons in which we live. Give them the wisdom to lead and navigate the Church through the unique trials and difficulties of this generation. Lead them by the Holy Spirit's voice.

Bless each forerunner that you are preparing to be a voice of truth and righteousness that rings clear!

In the matchless name of Jesus,

AMEN!

CHAPTER 3

THE PURPOSE OF THE WILDERNESS

Embracing the Divine Season of the Wilderness

And the child continued to grow and to become strong in spirit, and he lived in the deserts until the day of his public appearance to Israel. (Luke 1:80)

All those who lived in the hill country of Judea heard about the miraculous signs that surrounded the birth of John the Baptist. Naturally, they were in awe and wonder of who John would turn out to be because the hand of the Lord was upon him at his birth. They were speculating and talking about what God was going to do with John. It's as if John had so much potential given the calling of God.

[65]Fear came on all those living around them; and all these matters were being talked about in all the hill country of Judea. [66]All who heard them kept them in mind, saying, "What then will this child turn out to be?" For the hand of the Lord was certainly with him. (Luke 1:65-66)

At some point in John's childhood, possibly when his parents passed away, John broke away from the expectations and traditions of Judaism to become a priest in the same order as his father Zacharias. Instead, John was most likely raised by the Essene community in the deserts of Judea. The Essenes were a sect of Judaism who willingly separated themselves and lived in the deserts to pursue a life of holiness away from the corruption of the religious system. It is probable that John grew up in this type of environment with these values. Whether it was John's own choice or the situation he was put in, he grew up in the wilderness separated from the priesthood of his fathers. It was as though John had thrown away all the potential and calling of being a priest in his father's footsteps that surrounded his life by going into the wilderness. The wilderness though was God's chosen training ground for John.

MY INVITATION TO THE WILDERNESS

At the ripe young age of 24, with a bachelor's degree in hand and two years of training in Kansas City at Metro Christian Fellowship under the leadership of Mike Bickle, I moved to Sarasota, Florida, in September of 1999 with the desire to marry Jennifer and travel the nations preaching the Gospel of Christ with her! I was excited to have my entire future ahead of me with so many ministry connections and possibilities. I felt that truly the "sky was the limit!" As I was driving to Sarasota, the Lord spoke to me again. I heard, "You are going to have five years of death." When I heard it, it didn't register with me. I was familiar with the concept of dying to self, but I didn't have a paradigm or grid to understand what God was telling me. The wilderness was not a subject I had heard preached on; it's not a very popular message in our Christian culture. Nevertheless, the Lord was inviting me into the wilderness whether I liked it or not!

I had no idea of what I was heading into; I just wanted to serve the Lord and follow Him. I didn't have the perspective to understand what was happening as I moved to Sarasota. At the time it only felt like discipline from the Lord. All I could see was a time of stripping away my strengths, dying to the dreams and promises in my heart and actively waiting for God to do something! Anything! This wilderness period in my life lasted almost twelve years; as I look back now, I am so grateful for it.

AN INTRODUCTION TO THE WILDERNESS

From God's perspective, the wilderness seasons in the lives of His choice servants is not a new concept. From the time God gives His promises to the fulfillment of them, the wilderness has long been part of God's ways of preparing and raising up

His servants. Joseph waited 13 years, Abraham waited 25 years, Moses waited 40 years, David waited 20 years, Jesus waited 30 years, and Paul waited 12 years. *God strategically uses the wilderness for two primary purposes in our lives - to build intimacy with the Lord and to prepare our hearts.* There are areas of the human heart that can best be won over by love, shaped and revealed through the process of waiting and dying. God uses the wilderness seasons of our lives as the context to make the messenger into the message!

"Therefore, behold, I will allure her, bring her into the wilderness and speak kindly to her. (Hosea 2:14)

Now in those days John the Baptist came, preaching in the wilderness of Judea (Matthew 3:1)

The first and foremost purpose of the wilderness season is God's desire to draw us out to Himself so that we may encounter the passionate fire of His heart! Many times we think of the wilderness as a time of testing, pruning and waiting until we are prepared and ready for what God has for us. Some of this is true, but when we know God's heart we know His greatest desire and His primary purpose of the wilderness is for us to meet Him and find intimacy! Intimacy is established by spending time with the Lord and touching His unquenchable burning love. Whoever touches this love gets caught on fire!

This was John's story in the wilderness. John found a fire in the love of God that was more than enough. It not only sustained him, but also the love of God satisfied him! Beloved, this is what our hearts are crying out for - *a love so divine that it wins us over not just to work for God in ministry but an intimate jealous love that satisfies and defines us!* The good news is that this is the kind of love that God has for us. John entered into this intense desire of God's heart as he never left the "wilderness of desire" for the sake of his ministry. Instead, he preached and called Israel *to the wilderness* until he was taken to prison by Herod. John did not forsake his secret life with God for the sake of ministry but instead ministered from the overflow of intimacy. So much so that he did not leave the wilderness for the tradeoff of what we would call "the ministry." The "wilderness of desire" is not a means to an end, encountering the burning heart of God *is* our ultimate prize!

Solomon described it this way in Song of Solomon 8:5, "***Who is this coming up from the wilderness leaning on her beloved?***" This verse is such a beautiful description of the love and intimacy God releases in the wilderness. If we yield to the process of this divine furnace, our hearts will be set on fire for God in such a deeper way where we do come out of the wilderness "leaning on our beloved."

ISRAEL IN THE WILDERNESS

*[2]"Go and proclaim in the ears of Jerusalem, saying,
'Thus says the LORD, "I remember concerning you
the devotion of your youth, the love of your
betrothals, your following after Me in the wilderness,
through a land not sown. [3]"Israel was holy to the
LORD, the first of His harvest. All who ate of it
became guilty; Evil came upon them," declares the
LORD.'" (Jeremiah 2:2-3)*

We observe God leading the Israelites through the wilderness for forty years due to their disobedience. The journey to the Promised Land of Canaan that should have taken them a few weeks or months took them forty years as part of God's punishment. We look at Israel's behavior and reaction through their wilderness wanderings as negative; however, God's evaluation of events can be very different than ours. He reveals through Jeremiah the prophet how He interpreted the events of the wilderness (Jeremiah 2:2-3). The Lord was moved by Israel's devotion and desire to follow Him! The purpose for which He called her into the wilderness was to establish intimacy through the marriage covenant given through Moses. Thankfully, God doesn't define us by our outward actions but by our motives and desires. He did this with Israel in the desert, and He does it with us! But they were all there to die.

THE MUNDANENESS OF THE WILDERNESS

[2] "You shall remember all the way which the LORD your God has led you in the wilderness these forty years, that He might humble you, testing you, to know what was in your heart, whether you would keep His commandments or not. [3] "He humbled you and let you be hungry, and fed you with manna which you did not know, nor did your fathers know, that He might make you understand that man does not live by bread alone, but man lives by everything that proceeds out of the mouth of the LORD. (Deuteronomy 8:2-3)

One of the crucial aspects we encounter in the wilderness is the strength of our flesh! This obstacle is probably the strongest one we consistently face throughout our Christian lives. Our flesh and carnal desires are the most prominent hindrances to encountering God. Thankfully, the Lord uniquely designs each wilderness season so that we have to face ourselves. The routine and mundaneness during this season are to remove the distractions that fill our lives. Most people fill their lives with distractions to keep from having to deal with the real issues of their past, pain, disappointments, etc.; thus we never grow and mature beyond these issues. The Lord wants us to face ourselves including our greatest fears and hurts so that God can show Himself as the healer and the One that is greater than ourselves! If we will embrace this wilderness and not run away from it, we will find great healing and freedom!

There is another major area of carnal strength deeply embedded and hidden that needs to be revealed - especially in American Christianity. In this culture, where our individual dreams, callings, gifts, and abilities are touted, there has been a perverted view of what success looks like in God. We have adopted and integrated the worldly view of success and brought it into our spiritual lives with Christ so that success is defined by large numbers and bigger budgets. We espouse and buy into the idea, whether consciously or subconsciously, that success or maturity in God looks like "making it" into the Christian conference circuit, being a sought-after, renown worship leader or finally having a "platform" so that our names are known. These things aren't all bad; however, when this is modeled and propagated as the face of success or maturity, it becomes a source to feed our flesh and egos with Christian verbiage. What I mean by that is we hide behind these "Christian goals" to fulfill our selfish ambition and lust for fame, money, and power without even knowing it at times. In our modern American Christianity, we have lost not only the holiness of God and the fear of the Lord but also the sense of the "sinfulness of sin" (Romans 7:13) and the strength of our flesh and fleshy desires which cannot please God (Romans 8:8).

The mundaneness or the slowing down of our lives is necessary to reveal our desires. Fasting carries the same idea where we embrace voluntary weakness and time set apart so that we can have more of God and less of us. Essentially, God will starve us out so that we will listen to Him! Many times this season of mundaneness looks like being passed over for a position or seemingly set aside on the shelf as we wait for the Lord. These happenings are not a demotion or punishment as often thought, but it is actually God's jealousy over our lives to put us on His potter's wheel to shape and mold us into His image!

Another important aspect of the wilderness that many do not understand is the sense of loneliness. Many feel alone and yearn for someone to understand what they are going through. Some take this as punishment from God or want to run to other things and people from the sheer loneliness itself. They can't seem to put into words the various thoughts and emotions that swirl within them and constantly fight. They think, "If only I had someone I could talk to" or "I need someone to run with [in pursuing God] who understands me." Beloved, let me share a secret with you. The loneliness you feel is the Lord's doing! It is a sign that God's divine hand is upon you in this season! It is part of the wilderness so that you will find no other comfort but in the Lord Himself. Jeremiah lived through this and finally understood that God had set him apart. He says in Jeremiah 15:17, "***Because of Your hand upon me I sat alone.**"* What an amazing statement! Loneliness is part of the mundaneness of the wilderness. Don't despise it. Embrace it and take advantage of the time He has given you. It really is a blessing. You may never have another season of time like this again.

MY OWN WILDERNESS

I was enrolled at Regent Seminary in Vancouver, BC to start studying Greek right after my time in Kansas City but I felt the Lord leading me away from school. Instead (in September of 1999) I drove into Sarasota, Florida, with all that I owned packed into my car to be closer to Jennifer and to pursue her in marriage. I didn't know anyone in Sarasota, I didn't have a job, but Jennifer had arranged for me to stay with a family who had three young children. I had never even heard of Sarasota, and now here I was without any direction! I had not worried about making money or how I was going to live; I just assumed I was going to school to become a pastor. Now reality was setting in…

I got a job right away at Kilwins, a local ice-cream parlor at a fancy, tourist shopping spot on St. Armands Circle. Bank of America also hired me and was training me to be a personal banker. About three months into my job at Bank of America I realized there was not much money in the position, but I had friends that were doing well in Medical Transcription. I figured that I had a bachelor's in biology, already knew some medical terms and this job looked easy enough, so I quit Bank of America and went to a local trade school to learn Medical Transcription for nine months. Three months into my journey in Sarasota, I was attending a trade school for Medical Transcription, working part-time at Kilwins scooping ice-cream for $8 an hour, plus I got another part-time job at Charlie's Crab bussing tables at night. This seemed nothing like going to the nations preaching the Gospel!

Another huge factor in my wilderness season was that I became involved in the small church that Jennifer had grown up in. The elders loved God, and there was a genuine swirl of prophetic activity in this little 40-50 member church; however, there was a strong spirit of control that pervaded everything. There was also a recognized prophetess in the group who had her own agenda. I did not know any of this nor understand it. Looking back I was so naive!

The elders of the church wanted to meet with Jennifer and myself within the first week I arrived in Sarasota. They had received "prophetic words" about Jennifer (that she was in deception) while she was away in Kansas City. The elders didn't exactly know what the deception was, but for sure they felt that Jennifer and I should not be together. They said that we had not fulfilled our nine-month discipleship program correctly without dating, so we needed to do it over again. We wanted to "submit" to our elders and not be rebellious so we agreed with them to not date for nine months. I moved to Sarasota to be with Jennifer, but now we could not date. A couple of months later the elders brought us in again and said that we were talking to each other too much and not being separated enough, so now we were no longer allowed to even speak to one other!

This was my introduction to the wilderness. I could not talk to Jennifer, the one I loved and had moved to Sarasota for. I was going to trade school and working two part-time jobs trying to survive. I was bewildered. My dreams seemed like another lifetime ago. I had alienated myself from my friends and connections from Seattle and Kansas City trying to be on friendly terms with our leaders in Sarasota. I was not in a good situation, and I was plummeting.

Then the self-talk and mind games started. On Saturdays, I would open early at Kilwins and make hundreds of waffle cones before the front window as I watched "life" go by. For hours at a time and months, I beat myself up thinking I had done something wrong to be in this position. I would ask God what I had done wrong and why He was punishing me. I began to fall into depression and have thoughts of suicide which I had never entertained before. There were so many afternoons that I would go to a local park next to the bay and just scream and cry not understanding what was happening in my life. I was so confused not realizing that God was doing a work of grace in my heart in this wilderness.

The wilderness is crucial in that it is the divine context for God's discipline and preparation to produce humility and ultimate dependence upon the Lord. God does not lead His children through the wilderness years because He is mad at us, disappointed with us, or angry at us. It is not a punishment for our behavior or our choices. God does bring about judgment and redemption into the lives of His children for sin but that is not what we are talking about in this book when referencing the wilderness season.

It is very revealing to hear God's heart in why He led Israel on this route. There were certain things that God was after that only the wilderness could bring out and produce. Moses tells us in the book of Deuteronomy as he recaps the wilderness wanderings that the *Lord was both leading them and testing them at the same time.* We don't like the idea of God "testing us," but in His divine wisdom, God will lead us into these "testing" seasons to reveal and expose what has lodged away and hidden deep in our hearts. The word for testing in Hebrew has the idea of proving, or what the test will bring about or reveal. It wasn't a pass/fail type of test per se. Instead, it was a test to show what was in their heart. The Lord had an end goal in mind for Israel that He wanted them to understand when the forty years were finished. He wanted Israel to know all the different things that were in their hearts so that ultimately they would become dependent on the Lord. The Lord gives us these wilderness times as a gift to us if we embrace His leadership in them.

I want to add a word against discouragement for those who read these words, and it gives understanding to the wilderness season that you have gone through in the past - yet you feel like you failed in that season. Your experience was different and looking back you felt like you didn't give yourself to the "wilderness of desire." That time was marked by failures, difficulties, lots of complaining and quitting on God (at least in your heart) and times of engrossing yourself in other lesser things. It wasn't outright backsliding but not a fullhearted pursuit of the heart of God. In evaluating your past, you wouldn't describe it as "giving yourself to the Lord in the wilderness" or "submitting to God's ways to be formed and prepared." Instead, you feel like you just stumbled your way through. Now you're here!

First, I want to reassure you that *God evaluates our lives and our response much differently than we evaluate them.* He sees our hearts desire to follow Him and the "yes" in our spirits to obey Him - and He is overcome by our weak efforts. His heart is moved and thrilled beyond words that we would receive from Him and pursue Him in return, as weak as it may have seemed. We think we missed out on lessons and delayed the process. What we don't understand is that Jesus was working on the interior of our hearts which is so difficult to assess. Moreover, I believe that *you actually received what you needed if you are not offended by Jesus* - meaning you are still in love with Him, following Him and are excited about Him.

Second, your season of development was not wasted if you have continued to walk with Jesus. He is the only One who can **"make all things work for good to those who love Him"** (Romans 8:28). Remember, He is the master potter, and we are the clay. This was all part of the process, and He will use the seemingly broken pieces to weave and make His tapestry from our lives. Trust me. God is good at this! He knows what He is doing. It's what He does with weak and broken human beings who love Him! So don't consider yourself as being disqualified and take courage!

MY OWN DELIVERANCE

We finally married on October 20, 2001, almost two years after moving to Sarasota! I remember weeping as I watched Jennifer, so beautiful and elegant, walking down the aisle. All of the emotions of this last season seemed to break like a flood as I recalled God's faithful leadership in bringing us together. The Lord broke into our situation, spoke to those around us and brought unity to our church fellowship. There was exceeding joy as we celebrated our wedding day together. It was like a dream had come true!

On our way back home from our honeymoon, we got a call that our elders wanted to meet with the small bible study group that we attended. To give you some context, a few of our closest friends in the church had been meeting together in a small weekly bible study group that soon turned into gossiping and complaining sessions about our leaders. The elders wanted to confront and address this issue.

A week later on a Friday night, the seven of us who were part of this Bible study were sitting in a small circle with our three elders. As our pastor started addressing the issues I spoke up and asked him what he thought was going on with each person. I was speaking out of arrogance and trying to fight against them in pride. So he went around the room evaluating each person's strengths and weaknesses during that season. As he would point things out, I would think, "I can see those issues. I understand why they are having problems and in this meeting!" Then he came to me last and said, "But you Roger,

I am worried about you." I thought, "Why are you worried about me? I can understand why you would be worried about the rest of the group, but I'm fine! The issue isn't me." Now, I had a good relationship with my pastor with whom I had met with regularly when I first moved to Sarasota. He discipled me, and we would spend hours talking about his past, what he had learned in his journey and where he thought our fellowship and the church at large was going prophetically. The next few hours of that night are a bit of a blur to me.

As I was sitting there in my seat, the Holy Spirit intervened! The next thing I remember is falling to my knees as I began to weep. I came under the conviction of the Holy Spirit like I had never done before. The Lord started to expose my own heart to me. I began repenting of the jealousy I had of other's gifts, my selfish ambition and lust for authority, the platform and spotlight, the critical spirit that I carried and would use against people, and so much more. I confessed the most intimate/deepest secrets and thoughts that I thought were safe in my mind behind lock and key from everybody; however, when the Holy Spirit comes, He has a way to open us up, not to hurt us, but to cleanse us and set us free. This went on for about three hours that night as the Lord exposed my heart, broke off generational curses and set me free in His love!

Here is one story I have to share that really defined that night - My pastor knelt down next to me and began to whisper a word of knowledge that he was hearing. He said, "I hear the word 'pretty boy.'" When he said this, it was as if a sword went through my heart! Only my wife understood what this term meant to me and what was happening; it was truly a divine word of knowledge. Let me explain. I had used that term, "pretty boy" condescendingly to describe other guys that I thought were handsome, kind of like renaissance guys, who acted so arrogantly and were well put together. It was a false image in my mind that I envied and wanted to be like so I would use the term and throw it around out of jealousy and insecurity. Only Jennifer knew that! All of a sudden, the Lord was calling me a "pretty boy!" He was revealing that though I felt inferior and intimidated by these other guys, in my pride, that is the way I saw myself and what I wanted to become!

As I look back over the years of my journey this night stands out like a beacon of change and hope. The Lord sovereignly chose to meet me that night and set me free to be me. What I didn't realize or want to admit was that deep down I had secretly viewed myself as a "pretty boy" and my identity was wrapped up in this false idea and image. When this was exposed and repented of that night, I left so "light" even though I didn't know who I was. *My identity had been built on so many wrong ideas of myself that when they were taken out from under me, I had to begin to learn who I was in Christ!* This is real freedom!

THE WILDERNESS MINDSET

"Have I not commanded you? Be strong and
courageous! Do not tremble or be dismayed, for the
LORD your God is with you wherever you go."
(Joshua 1:9)

As I have met and talked with people on this journey, I have a particular burden for those, especially forerunners, who have been sidelined during the wilderness season of life. Many have given up on the call of God on their lives, while some have been derailed by the unexpected length or difficulties of the desert. What I find most devastating though is the wilderness mindset God's people walk around with. It is a defeated, hopeless, God-is-against-me and I'll-never-walk-in-the-full-promises-of-God attitude that permeates their outlook on life. Our churches are full of people like this. Somewhere along the trials and difficulties of life, their poor decisions and the consequences thereof, their spirits have been beaten down. If this is you, I want to encourage you that the end of your story has not been written yet.

Let me share with you about my wilderness mindset. The Lord began to speak to me and move us out to do more city-wide ministry towards the end of 2011. We had some initial success in gathering different churches and youth groups for various prayer initiatives, however, what we ultimately wanted was to establish a House of Prayer. As the burden for the House of Prayer grew, I had a major faith dilemma brewing inside me. I knew the charge for the House of Prayer was from the Lord; however, I had so much doubt, fears, and unbelief about how it could turn into a reality. I felt like there were chains that were tying me down from soaring into the promises of God. I realized that the shackles tying me down were "logic" and "reason." All the people I talked to said the same things to me, "How are you going to start a House of Prayer?", "You don't have any money to start a House of Prayer," and "You don't have any connections to start a House of Prayer." The problem was, I was agreeing with these people and living with the wilderness mindset; God can't use me because of all the issues. But in my heart, I felt trapped and was crying out, "Where are those who live by faith and not by sight? Those who soar in the promises of God!?" Finally, the struggle came to a head, and I had to make a decision. Do I live by what I can't do or don't have, or do I trust God and go for it? I would rather go for it and fail than play it safe, never go after my dreams and live with regret. At some point in your life, you will have to "go for it" and trust God.

Our Jesus is the God of hope (Romans 15:13) and causes all things to work for good to those who love Him (Romans 8:28). Be strong and courageous and risk again to press into God and hear His voice over you and your life afresh. Find a small community of believers you can trust who are pursuing God and throw yourself into it. Let their faith rub off on yours and begin to lift your spirits. Take the grave clothes off, take the wilderness mindset off and put on the new self, as Paul said in Colossians 3:10. Begin to walk in your true identity in Christ! Get back in the race and make your life count!!!

KEY UNDERSTANDING

From the testimony of the Scriptures, we see that God's optimal training ground is the wilderness! He leads His choice servants into seasons of the wilderness to gain our undivided attention. Here God wins over our hearts by revealing His passionate love for us. Our jealous Bridegroom yearns for us to be fully satisfied in having just Him. No other loves. No other gods.

God also uses the context of the desert to expose our hearts so that He can purify it and form it. We must begin to understand the different ways of God in the wilderness so that we do not get offended nor disillusioned and undercut God's plan of preparation. In submitting to God's plan, *we will walk out of the wilderness leaning on our beloved* (Song of Solomon 8:5)!

A PRAYER FOR FORERUNNERS

Father of Glory,

Thank you that you know us intimately and love us with an everlasting love! Thank you for Your divine wisdom in how You lead our lives. You know exactly what to allow in our lives and what to withhold and the proper times.

I pray for all those find themselves in this wilderness season in their lives. Thank you for their "yes" to follow You into the wilderness! Jesus, come and draw near to strengthen their hearts and give grace to their resolve. May they not quit the journey that You have divinely put them on. Lord, come and speak Your words of life and comfort to them today. Overcome every part of their lives by Your love.

I declare over these that they are the "favored ones in all the earth!" Now set your grace upon them to be able to willingly climb up on Your altar to lay down their lives, that You would kill what needs to die so that You may resurrect by Your Spirit every part of their lives. Let resurrection power reign over each these precious ones!

In the lovely name of Jesus,

AMEN!

CHAPTER 4

JOHN'S MESSAGE

Prepare the Way of the Lord

²The word of God came to John, the son of Zacharias, in the wilderness. ³And he came into all the district around the Jordan, preaching a baptism of repentance for the forgiveness of sins (Luke 3:2-3)

While John was communing with God in the wilderness, the Bible tells us that the Word of the Lord came to him. Interestingly, John did not start his ministry preemptively or presumptuously on his own accord; he waited for the directive of the Lord. The testimony of the Bible is that the word of God came to John while in the wilderness and *then* he began preaching a baptism of repentance, but still in the desert around the Jordan.

John's forerunner message was simple and focused - he was to prepare the way of the Lord which meant that he was to prepare the people to meet God. This was his assignment and commission. John's primary purpose was to be a witness, a testimony or a bridge that would bring people, not to himself or to grow his ministry, but to the One who was coming after him. He had a profound understanding of his place in God's redemptive plan. He also had an unusual ability to understand both his assignment but also his limitations. John knew that he was not the one who would bring salvation or deliverance to Israel (as much as they loved him). Instead, he knew that the One coming after him was *the Lamb of God who would take away the sin of the world* (John 1:29). *It is imperative that we understand our assignment from the Lord and the role that we play.* In it, our weaknesses as much as our strengths must be submitted to the Lord so that he can use us to His fullest extent.

REPENTANCE IS THE WAY OF PREPARATION

The way John prepared the hearts of the people of Israel was calling them to a place of repentance. John knew that being ready meant they would have to make room in their hearts for Jesus. Usually, people are so full of the appetite of the world they have no room for Jesus. At times, people's inability to grow is not always due to lack of spiritual desire but because they have no space in their lives and hearts to give to Jesus. Our hearts, minds, and emotions can be saturated with the world's values and goods so much so that we do not have room for God. Thus, many believers carry heavy weights and yokes that are symptomatic of the carnal, unrenewed minds that are overwhelmed with the desires and thoughts of this age. The key to breaking the agreement with the enemy and the spirit of this age is repentance! Repentance is a legal work which we control that breaks our voluntary cooperation with the enemy. It is more than just confession and turning from our sin. In the powerful work of repentance, we access the power of the cross to identify ourselves as the one who Christ died for, thus coming under the headship of Christ in breaking off our ties with the devil. It is not a dirty word nor is it old fashioned and out of style. Rather, I believe our modern Christian culture has lost the power and joy of repentance which prepares us to encounter Jesus in new and fresh ways!

This power and joy is exactly what John offered to the religious group in his day. Matthew tells us that "***Jerusalem was going to him, and all Judea and all the district around the Jordan***" (Matthew 3:5). John was a religious phenomenon and the people were flocking to experience him. He baptized that generation, up to 1.5 million Jews, with the baptism of repentance so their hearts would be prepared to receive the forgiveness of sins offered by the Lamb of God. I believe that God will once again send a wave of repentance to our nation and our generation in His mercy because it is through entering into this repentance that strongholds and strongmen are exposed and broken. This genuine, Holy Spirit-led, convicting-of-hearts type of repentance that God offers is the key to receive more of what Jesus offers - cleansing of sin, healing of hearts, empowerment by grace and much more. Godly repentance will also break and eradicate the enemy's bondage in our lives, our families, our churches and our cities. In the humility of confessing and repenting, we identify with the need of the blood of Jesus and then appropriate that same power of the blood against the forces of darkness.

FRUITS OF REPENTANCE

"Therefore bear fruits in keeping with repentance, and do not begin to say to yourselves, 'We have Abraham for our father,' for I say to you that from these stones God is able to raise up children to Abraham. (Luke 3:8)

John didn't stop his message with repentance alone; He taught men to bear the fruits of repentance. The goal of repentance or turning away from sin is more than just a one-time decision. Long-term freedom comes from deciding to turn away from sin and to return to God over and over again. In doing so, we bear the "fruits of repentance." I believe the Lord is after more than just our acknowledgment of sinful and wrongful patterns in our lives though this is important. Acknowledgment is the starting point to freedom, but acknowledgment is not enough. Over the years I have seen many believers who are great at analyzing their "issues" and talking to others about them in a weird, masochistic type of way, yet they never seem to be able to make the small choices that actually bring liberty. John's message of repentance is an invitation for freedom in our lives! Liberty begins by repenting of our sins but is worked out in our lives by walking in righteousness. It is making the small, right choices when no one sees us (over and over again) because we are cognizant that we live before an audience of One who sees all things! This is called living in wisdom or living by the fear of the Lord. Establishing our lives in righteousness is how we bear fruits in keeping with repentance. Repentance closes all legal rights to the devil, and walking in righteousness **keeps** the door closed so the devil cannot come back in. The truth that the enemy does not want you to know is that you have great authority over your own soul and spirit. The enemy can attack and distract us from the outside, but cannot hinder us internally. It is our own cognitive choices between whether we live as slaves of sin or slaves of righteousness (Romans 6) that determines if we open the door to let the enemy into our lives. He may threaten us, but we ultimately have the power over our souls in the redemption of Christ. It is in bearing the fruits of repentance that *we are being changed from glory to glory* (2 Corinthians 3:18) and are gaining victory as we become more like Christ.

And the crowds were questioning him, saying, "Then what shall we do?" (Luke 3:10)

On three separate occasions in Luke 3, as John is teaching about repentance, the crowds ask him "what shall we do?," or how does the fruit of repentance look? John gives different practical answers in Luke 3 about sharing your tunic and your food (v. 11), only collecting the right amount of taxes (v. 13), being content with your wages (v. 14) and not stealing.

Essentially, John is teaching them to live with an opposite spirit than the world, returning good for evil. He is likening the fruits of a repentant lifestyle with the lifestyle that Jesus would later teach called the Sermon on the Mount (Matt 5-7).

THE SECRET TO JOHN'S PREACHING

We only have a few quotations of John's messages in the Bible. From what we do have we see John quoted the Old Testament as the foundation of his preaching: His teaching and preaching were not new or revolutionary in its content; instead, it was actually based on the same Biblical foundation as many rabbis who had taught and preached. What made John stand out so that his preaching would shake the nation? It was the anointing, or power of God, on his preaching. It wasn't just about the content, though that is important; John carried an authority where the Holy Spirit moved on the hearts of men while he spoke. *This type of anointing cannot be earned or bought but is birthed foremost from a place of intimacy with God.* In other words, John was saturated in the Word of God and God Himself! One of my favorite quotes I heard years ago is "messages born in the mind reach the mind, but messages born in the heart reach the heart." This is so true. Preaching is not only about disseminating the right information; it is more about conveying the heart and mind of God which requires experiential personal knowledge. When we begin to enter into this type of preaching, the Holy Spirit confirms both the message and the messenger by releasing His conviction and authority. This is how John carried his heart and preached the word of God with fire. The fire of God's word drew the hearts of men so they would willingly take the arduous journey into the wilderness to witness and encounter the anointing that John carried.

¹Now in those days John the Baptist came, preaching in the wilderness of Judea, saying, ²"Repent, for the kingdom of heaven is at hand." (Matthew 3:1-2)

From that time Jesus began to preach and say, "Repent, for the kingdom of heaven is at hand." (Matthew 4:17)

John came on the scene preaching a message of repentance for the time of the breaking in of the kingdom of God had come. John, the forerunner, preached the identical message that Jesus would proclaim when He began His ministry after coming out of the wilderness. There is a massive nugget of insight for us to glean from these two passages in Matthew 3 and Matthew 4. John the Baptist gives us a clear principle in John 3:27 when he *"answered and said, 'a man can receive nothing unless it has been given him from heaven.'"* So the repentance message that John was preaching in the wilderness was not something that he thought of or brought about, it was actually given from heaven. This reality was validated as true when Jesus began His ministry by preaching the same fundamental and literal message, and we know that Jesus received it from Heaven as He was the one who came from *"the bosom of the Father"* (John 1:18). This tells us that *genuine forerunners who stand in the presence of God in the secret place will receive the same burden or message in our day that Jesus carries!* Jesus is burdened over the sin and corruption of our generation. I believe He stands before us and our generation as He did when He stood outside Jerusalem in Luke 19:41 and Matthew 23:37 and wept over the city longing to gather the people to Himself. Even now Jesus longs to rescue and deliver the nations from the torment of sin and the devil. If we are in tune with the heartbeat of God, we can hear the cry of Jesus in the message of the end-time forerunners who God is beginning to raise up.

ZEAL FOR THE TRUTH

For John had been saying to him, "It is not lawful for you to have her." (Matthew 14:4)

John the Baptist was confronting Herod Antipas for taking his brother Philip's wife, Herodias. Matthew tells us in Chapter 14, verse 4, that John "had been saying" this to them, meaning that this was not the first time he brought this up. Mark's gospel in Chapter 6 reveals that Herodias actually was "holding a grudge" against John and wanted to put him to death. These passages show that John had been confronting this immoral action of incest for some time now which was forbidden by the law (Lev 18:16). John had the boldness and confidence to confront the ruler of his region, or the equivalent of the king of a nation, about his immoral behavior in his personal life. Many in our generation will have this same opportunity to confront leaders and rulers against their lifestyle of sin and immorality. The question is, what will we say when we stand before them? Will we shrink in fear of man or rise to the challenge in fear of the Lord? John understood that speaking against Herod could mean his life, but he did not back down from the truth. Where did John get this boldness?

I believe John had a zeal for the truth as he personally experienced the Word of the Lord coming to him in the wilderness (Matthew 3:2). John was tenacious for righteousness as he preached against the hypocrisy of the Pharisees and the lowering of the standard of righteousness in his day. *The truth itself has authority for us to stand in.* When John confronted Herod with the truth, he was elevating the rule of the Word of God as the standard by which both believer and unbeliever must give account. The Word of God has full and final jurisdiction over every person who has been born. It is the measuring rod against which the intents and actions of every person will be measured. In confronting those who are in sin against the Word of God, we are actually bringing them into an encounter with the Word. In other words, we are introducing them to the standard of the Word by which they will ultimately be judged. The standard will not be a secret to them in the day of judgment. We can only lay forth this type of standard to others when we have allowed the truth of the Word first to judge us. Hebrews 4:12 tells us that the Word of God is *"**living and active…and able to judge the thoughts and intentions of the heart**."* Allowing the living Word to judge and reveal our thoughts and hearts now is the context that produces confidence in our spirits so that we can bring that same standard to others. One of the primary things that God is calling us to and affording us in these preparatory days is to build our history with the Word of God by spending quality time in it. This feasting in the Word leads us to encounter Jesus, as the word of God always points us to the Son (John 5:39).

> *47"If anyone hears My sayings and does not keep them, I do not judge him; for I did not come to judge the world, but to save the world. 48"He who rejects Me and does not receive My sayings, has one who judges him; the word I spoke is what will judge him at the last day. (John 12:47-48)*

There is a widespread belief in the Christian world that believers "expect the heathen to act like a heathen" so we don't address their sinful lifestyles. The idea is that because they do not have the Holy Spirit living within them and are not born again, they do not have the ability to live holy. It is true that unbelievers do not have the power to overcome sin or live lifestyles of holiness; however, they are still held to the same standard of truth by which they will be judged. It is actually in raising the standard of truth to an unbeliever that disrupts and gives room for the Holy Spirit to bring conviction, hope and life. If we forsake unbelievers in their degenerate condition because they can't do anything about it or because it is uncomfortable to us, then we actually leave them trapped in their bondage to sin! Hope begins when we are confronted by the truth! This is the first act of mercy that God brings to any person's life. *It is the introduction to the transcendent truth that leads us to the God of Truth and actually begins to move us away from the temporal reality of our own perception of right and wrong enabling us to see truth from God's perspective.* The breaking in of the light of God's Word is a sword the cuts away deception and darkness if we will allow it. The hope of truth is God's mercy towards us!

THE COST OF STANDING FOR THE WORD OF GOD

John ended up paying the ultimate price for standing with the Word of God - his life. Herod beheaded John at the request of Herodias' daughter. As her daughter danced before the king, he was pleased and offered up to half of his kingdom. Herodias incited her daughter to ask for the head of John the Baptist on a platter; the king, in his embarrassment, responded immediately and John's head was carried into this dinner party on a silver platter for King Herod's guests to behold. As forerunners, we must be prepared to lay down our lives for the sake of standing with the truth. This doesn't mean that every forerunner will die as a martyr, but it does mean that we cannot shrink back against the lies that are being propagated by the devil into our culture. The enemy's agenda is to marginalize and mitigate away: the truth of God's word over the identity of Christ, the way of genuine salvation, the definition and purpose of the grace of God, and so many other crucial doctrines of the faith *"once for all handed down to the saints"* (Jude 3). These are now a battleground in our society.

It would have been easy for John to say to himself, "I'll talk to Herod later about this issue," or justify his way out of confronting Herod with the truth. He knew the possible repercussions and authority that Herod had to end his life; however, he kept bringing the truth to bear upon him, and John did not stop. Interestingly, Herod had John arrested while he was preaching in the wilderness. John's public ministry lasted approximately six months while he was in prison for upwards of two years. Note that John was locked up much longer than he was in ministry.

END TIME MESSENGERS

I believe that God is going to raise up an army of anointed, fearless, end-time preachers of the Word of God who will not back down from the pressures or threats of our culture. They will confront the powers of evil head-on in our present world. They will minister in the power of the Holy Spirit like John did to shake people and nations through their deliverance of the *rhema* Word of God. These forerunners, having been trained and raised in the crucible of the wilderness, have already died to their own self-will and self-righteousness and counted the cost ahead of them as they proclaim the Lord's heart. Their words - like arrows of truth - will be spoken like arrows shot out to hit the target under the Holy Spirit's unction and guidance. God in His mercy is raising up and equipping to release this army of end-time messengers to prepare the way of the Lord's second coming through the message of repentance. They will warn the kings and judges of the earth to *"worship the Lord with reverence and rejoice with trembling. Kiss the Son lest He be angry and you perish in the way"* (Psalm 2:10-11). God has already sent this type of prophetic proclamation into motion, as Jesus promised in Matthew 24:14, that the "gospel of the kingdom shall be preached in the whole world as a testimony to all the nations" before the end will come.

> *"This gospel of the kingdom shall be preached in the whole world as a testimony to all the nations, and then the end will come. (Matthew 24:14)*

The "gospel of the kingdom" is more than the offering of the forgiveness of sins through the cross of Christ, which is wonderful and so very necessary. It is much more than the watered down "gospel" of easy belief or the seeker-friendly message of just "adding Jesus to your life" or "give Jesus a try." Instead, this "gospel of the kingdom" is an aggressive proclamation of what is on the Father's agenda as He begins to transition the age to give His Son the nations, the inheritance He deserves (Psalm 2:8). The message of Matthew 24:14 is a call to repentance and a warning to the elites of the world. It is the proclamation that another king from another kingdom, Jesus, is preparing to come and to take His rightful place. The "gospel of the kingdom" is a warning to all the unrighteous leaders and rulers of this age that unless they repent another king is coming who will replace them. When this anointed proclamation goes out into the nations, it will accelerate the rage of selfish and arrogant leaders against the Church. This royal decree will fuel the end-time persecution against the Church as forerunners testify of the truth of Jesus the king in the same manner John testified before Herod. I believe this last missional thrust of the global Church with the right understanding of the "gospel of the kingdom" will "*hasten the coming of the Day of the Lord*" (2 Peter 3:2). The end-time forerunners are to rally and equip the Church with an understanding of the "gospel of the kingdom" as well as demonstrate it in their sphere of influence. The question we want to tackle is, "How can these forerunners stand in confidence before the face of evil in this last generation?" Our next chapter is critical in answering this question as we look at how God formed John's identity.

KEY UNDERSTANDING

John the Baptist was anointed to prepare his generation for the coming of Messiah through the preaching of the Word. He was immersed and saturated in the Word of God as evidenced by the content of his message. Submission to the Word and a love for the truth and nurtured an anointing on his preaching. Beloved, there is no substitute or shortcut if you are to be a clarion voice from Heaven to this generation.

John focused on preparing the heart through the message of repentance. We not only need to understand the joy, power, and freedom of repentance, it needs to be worked through our lives so that we are living in the fruit of it. Consecrated and holy forerunners will be the ones that prepare the Bride of Christ to be a *"holy and blameless...having no spot or wrinkle or any such thing"* (Ephesians 5:27) ready for the bridegroom.

A PRAYER FOR FORERUNNERS

Heavenly Father,

Thank You for your kindness that leads us to repentance. May we experience the joy of repentance and the confidence of righteousness. Lord, I ask You to raise up clean, holy vessels in this generation whose devotion and lifestyles cause the aroma of Christ to arise.

Thank You for the truth that is found in Christ Jesus. I pray that you would make each forerunner into the message itself through Your dealings in their lives. Cause them to be a voice in this generation and not just an echo. May You forge conviction deep within their souls so that when pressures increase, these would not fall back but shine even brighter!

Lord, I ask that You would cause Your Word to be sweet to each forerunner; that You would kiss their hearts by Your Word and romance them with Your Gospel. Immerse them in the truth that it would form the message within them!

In the wonderful name of Jesus,

AMEN!

CHAPTER 5

JOHN'S IDENTITY

A Voice of One Crying in the Wilderness

THE TEST OF PRAISE

**_Now while the people were in a state of expectation
and all were wondering in their hearts about John, as
to whether he was the Christ (Luke 3:15)_**

As John's ministry was growing in popularity with a
generation who was hearing his voice, there was a growing
expectancy about who John was. The people were beginning
to wonder if John could be the expected Messiah or Christ that
Israel had long hoped for. The fanfare around John's ministry
grew as God's promotion came. *It is essential to understand
that this promotion is a test from the Lord to see if we are*

grounded in our identity or if the praise of men will move us. Solomon warns us from long ago that at some point each person is "tested by the praise of men." Proverbs 27:21 says ***"The crucible is for silver and the furnace for gold, and each is tested by the praise accorded him."*** The seeming success or growth of influence is one of the hardest things for men to steward correctly. Success, power, and financial blessing will exaggerate our lusts and give an opportunity for the selfish desires that we have had all along to manifest itself. The determining factor of standing right before the Lord and before men in both success and hardship is if we know our identity; I mean our true Christ-given identity. Do we know who we are in God or is our identity determined by what men say about us? I do not believe that we can go any further in God than what we understand and receive as our identity to be *in Christ.* Our unbelief limits our growth and potential in Christ. John underwent the same test of success as his name spread throughout the region of Judea.

WHO ARE YOU?

This is the testimony of John, when the Jews sent to him priests and Levites from Jerusalem to ask him, "Who are you?" (John 1:19)

The question always comes down to "Who are you?" Who do you believe yourself to be? What is your identity and value based upon? The way we answer this fundamental question about ourselves will determine how we handle success, failure, and pressure. It will ultimately reveal if we put our trust in the Lord or if we are fighting to establish our own righteousness. Do we feel loved and accepted because of who we are in Christ and what He has already done for us, or because of what we can accomplish in our own strength?

As John's popularity grew among the contemporary religious Jews, they sent out priests and Levites to ask him this question - "Who are you?" This question also implied, "who gave you the authority to do what you do because what we do comes from who we are." Outwardly, John was baptizing in the wilderness. But the more pressing question was, who gave you the authority to baptize in the desert? This is the question they wanted an answer to.

> *[20]And he confessed and did not deny, but confessed, "I am not the Christ." [21]They asked him, "What then? Are you Elijah?" And he said, "I am not." "Are you the Prophet?" And he answered, "No." [22]Then they said to him, "Who are you, so that we may give an answer to those who sent us? What do you say about yourself?" (John 1:20-22)*

It is crucial to understand John's response. Before he went on to answer who he was, he begins by saying who he was not. He knew the traditional and cultural expectations and the lens from which the Jews were asking him. In Jewish tradition, there were different ones that the Jews were expecting that would come and bring deliverance to their people group. They were longing for the Messiah or the Christ. However, they also had an anticipation that Elijah would come back, even today they still do. Others believed a Prophet like Moses would come again to save Israel like in the days of old. John succinctly confesses that he is not any of these that they are expecting. There is a key lesson for us to learn here: *If we do not know who we are in Christ - our value, our assignment, our giftings, etc.; then we will conform into the identity expected of us from others.* We either take on the character that Christ gives us or we become conformed to the likeness that people expect of us. There is a third option, and that is the one we are born with - the fallen image of Adam. Naturally, we carry within us the slavery mindset of the old man and believe that is who we are though we have turned to Jesus. Both our Adamic image and pretenses put on us by others are false images of ourselves and need to be identified and torn down.

The old man is the sinful nature of Adam that is passed on to every person that is born. The apostle Paul describes this unredeemed condition in Ephesians 2:3 saying "**among them we too all formerly lived in the lusts of our flesh, indulging the desires of the flesh and of the mind, and were by nature children of wrath, even as the rest.**" Later, in the same letter to the Ephesians, Paul compares the "old man" enslaved in sin before Christ to the "new man" that is created through the born again process of salvation. **[22] That, in reference to your former manner of life, you lay aside the old self** [man]**, which is being corrupted in accordance with the lusts of deceit, [23] and that you be renewed in the spirit of your mind, [24] and put on the new self** [man]**, which in the likeness of God has been** *created in righteousness and holiness of the truth. (Ephesians 4:22-24).* When an individual gives their life to Jesus in repentance and faith, the greatest miracle takes place. Their old sinful nature is crucified with Christ (Romans 6:6) and exchanged for a new nature, the righteous nature of Christ. Thus believers are called *"new creatures in Christ"* (2 Corinthians 5:7). Many genuine born-again believers who have the imputed righteousness of Christ within them still carry around the old man mentality or belief system. Meaning, they still have the same thought process, lustful desires and mindsets as before they met Jesus. It is critical that we are able to identify our old ways of viewing ourselves, emotional patterns, ways of thinking, etc., and then renew or exchange them with the Word of God. This exchange is what allows us to walk in the power of the new man. This is called sanctification or being made more and more into the image of Jesus.

A central part of this growing process in sanctification is understanding how we think of ourselves and where that identity comes from. Another way of saying it is, who forms our identity and how do we define success? What value system do we hold and live by? Is my persona defined by the Word of God or by what others say and think? Many have spent their entire lives trying to live up to other peoples' expectations or the desire to be like someone else only to be shipwrecked and disillusioned when this mirage comes crashing down. Because John knew who he was, he immediately understood who he wasn't! Do you know who you are? Are you being defined by what others are expecting of you? Are you establishing your identity by what you can accomplish or want to be?

KNOWING OUR IDENTITY

He said, "I am a voice of one crying in the wilderness, 'make straight the way of the Lord,' as Isaiah the prophet said." (John 1:23)

John's answer about himself is so profound that it cannot be understated. What I love about John's response is that he identified himself as what the Word of God declared about him. He understood who he was from the truth of the Biblical testimony. John was clear that he was the forerunner before Jesus and that his assignment was to "make straight the way of the Lord!" John had spent so much time with the Word that the Word determined his identity. In other words, he didn't just repeat and echo what Isaiah the prophet said; he *became* what Isaiah prophesied. The truth of the Word of God gives us an understanding of who we have become in the new birth.

Many things happened in our hearts and minds when Jesus purchased us through the payment of His blood. We became born again by the Spirit (John 3:3) and became a new creature in Christ (2 Corinthians 5:17). Theologically, this is called justification where our sins are paid for and forgiven, and Christ's imputed righteousness is given to us. This becomes our new identity as Jesus purchases our lives by the price of His blood (1 Corinthians 6:20).

However, we do not immediately understand all that God has done for us in Christ Jesus, and it takes the revelation of the Word of God through study and meditation to tap into who we truly are. Another way of saying this is that *the truths of God's Word reveals to us what happened in salvation and the Word gives expression and understanding to what we already have and feel.* It's comparable to someone giving us the keys to a million dollars tucked safely away in the bank. However, if we don't know how much we have or how to access the money, it is useless to us though it is sitting there with our name attached to it! The Word of God reveals to us how much we have and how to access the precious gift of salvation and new *zoe* life that was given to us through the Cross.

MY ENCOUNTER WITH THE WORD OF GOD

I met Jesus as a confused and hurting 20-year-old sophomore at the University of Washington, and my heart was lit on fire. However, I had many wounds that I was carrying from my past that I did not understand. My father had passed away in a car accident when I was 10 years old. He left on a Saturday morning, and he never came back. This tragic incident shook the foundation of our family and my life. Layers of anger, unbelief towards God and walls of protection were built to survive through my teenage years. Beyond the arrogant and cocky exterior I portrayed, there was an insecure 10-year-old boy who simply wanted to be loved and nurtured. This was still the state of my heart after finishing college as I went to Master's Commission in Kansas City.

As part of our program in Master's Commission, we had to answer questions from a book called *"The Search for Significance"* by Robert McGee. I remember writing my answers in my journal and then re-reading them. As I was reading a description in my answer, I suddenly realized that I did not like the person it was representing. The problem was I was describing myself! This was the first time that I had encountered myself objectively, and I did not like it! So, I did what any mature 20-year-old believer in Jesus would do, I closed my journal and acted as if I had never written or read my entry. At that time I had no grid for these issues or even how to begin to deal with it. I chose to continue to live behind my wall of protection.

The following week during our home group, we had another set of questions we had to answer from the same book. Again, the same thing happened. As I began to read my description of myself, I was in shock and disbelief to see the person that I was. This time though, I didn't close my journal and run. Instead, I began the journey of facing myself! Often, this can be the hardest journey of all. With the help of my leaders and our class, I began to see my wounds, pain and insecurities and some of the ways that I would deflect them or cover them up. My primary assistant in my journey to find healing was the Word of God. I would look myself in the mirror every morning and say, "I am loved, and I am a lover of God" even though I had trouble believing that God loved me. By raw faith, I would pray and speak the Word of God over myself. As I did this for months, I began to encounter the living Word that slowly renewed my mind and transformed by heart. This new practice catapulted my journey in finding my identity in Christ.

THE POWER OF THE WORD OF GOD

Death and life are in the power of the tongue, and those who love it will eat its fruit. (Proverbs 18:21)

This is what I have learned over the years of walking alongside others through this journey of healing - the most authoritative voice over your life is YOU! It's not your parents, a preacher or even the devil. Instead, you are the one who speaks words of life or words of death over yourself hundreds of times a day without even knowing it. You have the power to bless or the power to curse yourself, and you utilize that authority every day of your life. God wants to redeem that authority so that we align and submit ourselves to the Word of God and speak life, blessing and freedom over ourselves and others.

The enemy does not play fair and will use whatever means possible to get into people's lives - especially in their childhood. He will take advantage of a tragedy or a crisis in our lives and use it as a foothold to get into our hearts. Though the enemy cannot control our response or make us get angry, bitter or vengeful, he can use others to hurt us. All kinds of mistreatment from others is done to us as children to wound us, including physical, emotional and sexual abuse. When this happens, in our natural response, we react in sin of all sorts like anger, rage, etc. The principle is: when we sin it legally opens the door to allow the enemy to come in. The enemy provokes us by using other people's actions against us so that we respond in sin; when we do, the enemy comes and builds a stronghold in our lives. These strongholds affect the way we think, view life, respond emotionally, and how we see God and ourselves.

Another seemingly benign tactic that the devil uses are curses and words. I'm sure you have heard the famous children's rhyme, "Sticks and stones may break my bones, but your names will never hurt me." Well, sticks and stones may break our bones, but words **will** break our spirits, emotional states, and mindsets. In many ways, words are more powerful than physical actions. Proverbs 18:21 says "***Death and life are in the power of the tongue.***" Remember, in the beginning God used "words" to create everything - He spoke, and it was done! That is how powerful words are. *A fundamental principle used for both good and evil is that given time, our emotions will follow what's said whether it's true or not.* Over time, lies will bring about emotional trauma and depression, but the truth will bring about freedom. The devil knowing this uses people to speak lies and curses over us. Now, most of the time the people expressing these lies are talking out of their own woundedness and hurt, but they still throw these darts of death. Sometimes they are couched in sarcasm and humor. Other times they are very direct and aggressive. The aim, however, is the same - to pervert the way we think and feel about ourselves.

The worst part of the enemy's tactic is that gradually we come into agreement with what the enemy is saying over us and to us (through people), and he no longer has to shoot his lying arrows against us; we do it for him. Let me give you an example. A harsh and critical father makes comments to his son for years saying, "You're dumb," and "you'll never amount to anything," or to his daughter, "you're fat and ugly" and "no one will ever marry you." At first, we may disregard these lies, but when these same statements are made over us hundreds and thousands of times, we not only begin to believe them, but we actually begin to repeat them! We have now bought into the lie. Once this happens, we now start to curse ourselves, and the enemy has got us in this stronghold. We then continue for the rest of our lives with false views and self-pronounced curses that are empowered by our **own** voice until the power of God breaks in. This causes many warped and ungodly opinions of ourselves, unhealthy emotional states, broken spirits and wrong mindsets. This results in an endless amount of traffic in our minds and hearts that ends up blocking the voice of God! This is one of the red flags to identify these types of strongholds that exist in our lives. I have met so many people over the years who have genuine anointings and callings upon their lives and are being used by God in varying degrees, yet they have not broken the stronghold off their minds to fly free into their true identity in Christ!

The Lord wants a generation that is free of the oppression of the enemy in every respect where we can "*love the Lord our God with our minds, hearts, strength, and soul* (Matthew 22:37)!" One of the major components of this freedom is learning and understanding what Christ has done for us. Encountering God in His Word begins to transform the way we think and feel about ourselves. John the Baptist engaged with the Word in the desert so much so that his identity became the prophetic word that Isaiah proclaimed. John was bold in his stance that he was *"a voice of one crying in the wilderness, 'Make straight the way of the Lord,' as Isaiah the prophet said"* (John 1:23).

God wants us to be immersed in His Word so that we too may find our identity through the Word of God. For most, this is a process. I remind people that strongholds in their minds through believing lies are not created overnight. They are established over years and even decades. Freedom through the truth of God's word does not always come instantly. It may not take years, but there is a process of renewing our minds as Paul states in Romans 12:2. *The key is positioning ourselves in the Word of God to renew our minds.* It doesn't sound heroic nor is it even difficult, but many do not speak the Word over themselves and cut short the process of being healed and changed. If you continue this process, you will experience the power of God in His living Word and find the freedom you have earnestly sought!

PRACTICAL WAYS TO ENCOUNTER
THE WORD OF GOD

Let me share a few simple, practical tools to engage with the Word of God and find freedom:

First, make a time commitment. Understand at the beginning that your journey is precisely that, a journey! Make a minimum six-month commitment from the outset that you will continue to engage your heart. Set a time each day, even five minutes, where you will speak the Word of God over your life. Most of the failures in finding our identity in the Word of God is because we quit too early. God loves the process of our reach towards Him and His meeting us as we seek Him. The condition of your heart and quality of your life is a weighty matter and should be a priority. Do what it takes to schedule a few minutes each day to engage with the Word of God. You owe it to yourself!

Second, speak the truth of the Bible over yourself. It can also be called praying the Bible or pray-reading the Bible. This is a lot easier to do than it sounds. In whatever area you want freedom in, find Bible verses that speak truth to that area. Then each day, speak these verses out loud over yourself putting your name in it; make it personal. This is God's Word to you! Do this even if you don't believe it. Remember, your emotions will follow the truth.

Let me give you a simple example. Everyone knows John 3:16, *"For God so loved the world, that He gave His only begotten Son, that whoever believes in Him shall not perish, but have eternal life.*" Take this promise and speak it over yourself. Pray or speak the first portion of this verse. Here is what I said many times during my season of healing. *"For God, you so loved me, Roger, that you gave your only begotten Son to me."* That's it! As you speak this out loud (it has to be out loud so you can hear your voice) you will begin to create a dialogue with God.

Here is another verse that I prayed over myself often - 2 Corinthians 5:21, **"He made Him who knew no sin to be sin on our behalf, so that we might become the righteousness of God in Him."** I would pray, *"Thank you Lord that you have made me, Roger, the righteousness of God in Christ Jesus. I have received the righteousness of God through the work of Your Son. I stand before You, even now, clothed with your perfect righteousness."* These are simple prayers that you can say throughout the day when you have a one-minute break. It realigns your heart and mind back to God over and over again. It seems so simple to us, and it is, but I tell you the truth, God sees it as us loving Him through the Word and He responds in incredible ways towards us!

Third, meditate on the Word. Take a passage or phrase from a verse and repeat it and think about it over and over again throughout the day. Meditate in the Hebrew means "to mutter." The idea is that you chew on the truth and as you do, God will speak to you and direct you. The command to the Israelites in the Old Testament was actually to meditate on the Word day and night. (Joshua 1:8; Psalm 1; Psalm 27:4; Psalm 119:15, 48, 78, 148). I have found that meditating on the

Word of God is where revelation, insight, and transformation takes place, both in the mind and the heart.

Finally, keep a journal. Write out the prayers that you speak over yourself, the verses that you meditate on and the insights you receive as you do this. Over time, God will build a vocabulary with you for which you can dialogue with Him. Most people get bored in prayer because they don't know what to pray or run out of things to pray. Usually, the problem is because they don't have a vocabulary with God. As you pray and meditate on the Word, we build genuine intimacy with God, and He gives us an expression of that intimacy through our own history with Him.

I want to encourage you to set time aside to seek God in His Word in this particular way. Western Christianity has long championed Bible knowledge and the amount of the Bible we read, that is why there are so many "Read the Bible in One Year" programs. This isn't bad at all. However, biblical knowledge carries with it the idea of experiencing what you know or experiential knowledge. Applying this to the Bible means going "deep" in the truth of the Bible and not just reading for distance or length. When we dig through the outers crust into the depths of the Holy Scriptures, there is a river of magma available that will ignite your heart and transform your mind. Beloved, my prayer for you is that you recognize the lies of the enemy and position yourself to begin to encounter the fire of God's Word!

KEY UNDERSTANDING

Our identity in Christ must be formed by the truth of the Word of God. In doing this, we learn both who God says we are and who we are not; both of these are important to grasp. If we do not know who we are in Christ, we will allow the world and the society, even the Christian culture, to shape our value systems. If we are unfamiliar with the Biblical narrative over our lives, we will by default follow the secular story, and become sidetracked from who and what God has called us to be and do. *I don't believe we can go any further in God than who we know ourselves to be in Christ.* This is how critical it is that our identity is determined by the Word of God.

A PRAYER FOR FORERUNNERS

Dear Heavenly Father,

I pray for the spirit of truth to come and expose the lies of the enemy that you, my reader, have believed. May the Word of God come and divide between your soul and your spirit to set you free. Lord, heal the wounds of every person reading this book as they begin to understand the ways of the enemy.

I pray for the Word of God to prevail over each one who has undergone trauma in their past. Renew the minds of these beloved saints and restore what the enemy has stolen. Father, in Your mercy cut away every vestige of lies and bondages that hold each one back from walking in the full purpose of God. I ask that each one would genuinely know their identity in Christ without confusion and doubt. Give them confidence in Your love to be able to stand before You and men.

In the powerful name of Jesus,

AMEN!

CHAPTER 6

THE GLOBAL PRIESTHOOD

The Value of Ministry to the Lord

A STRATEGIC ENCOUNTER

[8]Now it happened that while he was performing his priestly service before God in the appointed order of his division…[11]And an angel of the Lord appeared to him, standing to the right of the altar of incense.
(Luke 1:8, 11)

The all-wise God who knows and understands all things could have met Zacharias, John's father, at any time to give the announcement of the forerunner. John was more than a son; he was a prophetic sign to his generation and a prototype for the last generation. Knowing the significance of John's calling, God sent Gabriel to meet Zacharias "while" he was performing his priestly service in the temple. The timing and importance of this encounter has tremendous global and eschatological implications that we need to understand in our day. The encounter with Zacharias is not a secondary point that can be overlooked.

It is a profound prophetic statement that God chose a priest to be the forerunner to prepare the way of the Lord. Furthermore, the announcement came while his father was offering the incense at the altar! Ironically, John served as a priest in a more genuine sense than the priesthood who served in Jerusalem and ministered in the temple. The combination of Gabriel's strategic appearance and announcement (he only announced two births in the entire Bible) and the fact that Gabriel came while Zacharias was offering incense in his priestly role signifies the importance of this event. I believe God was making an emphatic statement for those who have eyes to see about the primary priestly role that will permeate the forerunner ministry. *The forerunner ministry has its foundations in the priestly identity and therefore must operate out of that role.* Furthermore, this heavenly statement by God in divinely sending Gabriel while Zacharias was at the altar prophesies that the end-time forerunners will build and minister at the global altar as part of the preparation for the outpouring of the Holy Spirit, as well as the return of Christ.

PRIESTLY MINISTRY TO THE LORD

The role of the priest was established by the Lord as He called the Israelites out of Egypt. The priesthood was instituted in the wilderness as God drew near and established His covenant with the chosen nation. Aaron and his sons (Exodus 28:1) were set apart as the family line in Israel who would give themselves to the things of God full time. Serving God was both their occupation and their inheritance.

"You shall speak to all the skillful persons whom I have endowed with the spirit of wisdom, that they make Aaron's garments to consecrate him, that he may minister as priest to Me. (Exodus 28:3)

The purpose of the priesthood first and foremost was to minister to the Lord. They were set apart, consecrated in their occupation and their function so that they could give their full attention to the Lord. Included in ministering to the Lord was serving in the tabernacle and then the temple, but this was always understood to be secondary. In God's jealousy, the priests were set apart for Himself first! This consecration is in alignment with what He said when He delivered the entire nation of Israel out of Egypt so that they would be His *"own possession among all the peoples"* (Exodus 19:5). You hear God's desire as He says, *"and you shall be to Me a kingdom of priests and a holy nation"* (Exodus 19:6). God desires the entire nation would be given to Him in intimacy and consecration. This priestly intimacy is the primary relationship that God wanted with Israel, and what He wants with us. We will see later in this chapter how God revealed what ministry to the Lord looks like and how we as forerunners are to participate in that expression.

As religion crept in and the hearts of men grew cold, the priesthood of Israel became corrupt; meaning, they were doing it for their gain and not prioritizing the ministry to the Lord. This corruption began shortly after Aaron and his sons were set apart. His sons were consumed by the fire of God as they offered strange fire before the Lord (Leviticus 10:1-2). This continued through the generations as God brought glimpses of revival and reformation through the likes of Samuel, Zadok, and others.

What separated priests (Levites) from the other tribes of Israel is that they had exclusive access to or standing with God. This is why only the priests could set up and tear down the Mosaic tabernacle, carry the Ark of the Covenant, which represented the presence of God, or enter into the holy of holies on the Day of Atonement. *God's order from the beginning is that the priesthood who had unique access to God would both invite the Lord and bring about His presence.* In the New Covenant, the priesthood of all believers is the only privileged group allowed to stand in the Holy Place, which is not on the earth but in the heavenly temple through the blood of Christ (Hebrews 10:19-20). The priesthood becomes the mediator which connects God and Man, Heaven and Earth.

The priests, by their duties, would invite the Lord's presence on behalf of Israel against their enemies. We see this when the priests would carry the Ark of the Covenant on their shoulders into battle to bring about God's victory, like when the Lord sent the priests bearing the ark before Israel to bring down the walls of Jericho by the shout (Joshua 6). Even David would visit Nob (1 Samuel 21) for the priests to "inquire of the Lord" for him before he would go into battle on behalf of King Saul. In this same way, New Testament priests have the privilege and obligation to invite the Lord's manifestation in the midst of the darkness of this age. God has sent and established born-again believers as priests to draw His presence and to be a sign of the impending age to come. Remarkably, it is the Christian, and only the Christian, that points to Jesus in the midst of this perverse generation. The fact that believers are in any land is the commitment and tool through which God will break in with His Kingdom. The enemy is routed in geographic areas by the establishment of the Kingdom.

DAVID'S REVELATION AND VOW

²How he swore to the LORD and vowed to the Mighty One of Jacob, ³"Surely I will not enter my house, nor lie on my bed; ⁴I will not give sleep to my eyes or slumber to my eyelids, ⁵until I find a place for the LORD, a dwelling place for the Mighty One of Jacob." (Psalm 132:2-5)

David had a unique insight into God's heart about building a resting place on the earth, a habitation where the Lord can be with His people and receive ministry from them. In Psalm 132 we get to peer into David's heart and mind and see the revelation that drove him all the days of his life. As a youth on the hillsides of Bethlehem, while taking care of the sheep and worshipping the Lord, David received revelation that God wanted to establish a resting place on the earth, specifically in Zion or Jerusalem (v. 13). He made a vow in his youth that fulfilling God's desire would be his highest priority.

⁴David was thirty years old when he became king, and he reigned forty years…⁷Nevertheless, David captured the stronghold of Zion, that is the city of David. (2 Samuel 5:4, 7)

When David became king of all the tribes of Israel at age 37, he remembered the vow that he made to the Lord some 25 years ago of establishing the resting place. We know this because once David became King over all Israel and had authority to do whatever his heart pleased, the first assignment he carried out was capturing the stronghold of Zion and moving the capital of the nation there. It was as if David's dream had come true because he had been waiting all these years to establish Zion. Interestingly up to this time, Israel did not control Zion, and the land was barren. In essence, there was nothing desirable or significant about Zion other than the fact that the Lord had chosen it for Himself!

The next step in establishing the resting place of God was to bring the Ark of the Covenant to Jerusalem, which represented the presence of God. His first attempt in moving the ark ended up with the Lord's outburst of anger against Uzza (1 Chronicles 13) which frightened David so that he took the ark of God to Obed-Edom's house. This provoked David to search God's ways regarding the ark of God and more importantly, the priesthood. Three months later, David again gathered the nation and made a procession to bring the ark of God from Obed-Edom's house to Jerusalem. This time he followed the prescribed Levitical guidelines (1 Chronicles 15) on how to transport the ark. However, David, though he was king, also joined in welcoming the ark of God as a priest and offered sacrifices (1 Chronicles 15:27-16:3). With great joy they "**brought in the ark of God and placed it inside the tent which David had pitched for it**" (1 Chronicles 16:1).

God validates both priesthoods in this story. The Jews were still under the Levitical priesthood and had to follow it in transporting the ark to receive God's blessing. However, during the three-month break between the two attempts to bring the ark to Jerusalem, I believe David had a revelation of a superior, more ancient priesthood - the mystical priesthood of Melchizedek. David said in Psalm 110:4 "**The LORD has sworn and will not change His mind, "You are a priest forever according to the order of Melchizedek.**"

Melchizedek, king of Salem, was the one that the father of the Jews, Abraham, acknowledged and gave a tenth to in Genesis 14:20 signifying that the priesthood in Abraham's loins (the Levitical priesthood) was inferior to Melchizedek's (Hebrews 7). Interestingly, Jesus was from the line of Judah which is not priestly at all, but He identified Himself with Melchizedek just like David. We know that David's revelation of Melchizedek was correct and that God accepted it because God did not strike David down when he operated as a priest before the Ark of the Covenant. I believe this is why David was dancing with all his might in 1 Chronicles 15:29 as the ark of God came to the City of David. It was more than the ark coming! It was that David had heard God rightly, he aligned himself and had entered into this eternal priesthood.

In God's economy, priests are dynamically connected to the sacrifice they offer. The priesthood that King David operated in is the eternal and permanent priesthood of Melchizedek that Jesus also identified with. If David entered into this type of endless priesthood, it meant that the offering that he sacrificed is an eternal offering. I'm not talking about the eternal blood that Christ offered once and for all, but in the same order, the offerings of worship and prayer facilitated around the Ark of the Covenant night and day in the Tabernacle of David last forever! These sacrificial offerings of praise are treasured and remembered by God for all the ages.

Similarly, when we operate in our priestly identity, our spiritual sacrifices to God become eternal. Jesus has elevated the significance of our entire lives by grafting us into the eternal priesthood. No longer are we to differentiate between what is sacred and secular in our lives, instead, now everything we do is considered holy because our lives operate out of this perpetual priesthood. That means our work becomes sacred (Colossians 3:23-24), how we steward our relationships, and even what we eat (1 Timothy 4:5). The apostle Peter instructed us in this way, *"**We are being built up as a spiritual house for a holy priesthood, to offer up spiritual sacrifices acceptable to God through Jesus Christ** (1 Peter 2:5)."* Again, the offering is directly connected to the priesthood. If the priesthood is right and without end, then the offering becomes right and without end. If this is true, *what kind of holy lives do we need to live as it gives tremendous responsibility to our decisions?* The spiritual sacrifices of worship and prayer that we offer live forever, but our sacrifices include more than just these. The "sacrifice" encapsulates our entire lives, including our thoughts, motives, and actions. We know this because *God receives our offerings and rewards us in kind with imperishable rewards*! The eternal rewards given by God (1 Corinthians 3:11-15; 2 Corinthians 5:9-10) is the validation that our offerings and works remain forever. Beloved, this truth should put the fear of the Lord in us to live in such a way that honors the Lord!

THE TABERNACLE OF DAVID

⁴He appointed some of the Levites as ministers before the ark of the LORD, even to celebrate and to thank and praise the LORD God of Israel…³⁷So he left Asaph and his relatives there before the ark of the covenant of the LORD to minister before the ark continually, as every day's work required;
(1 Chronicles 16:4, 37)

David brought the Ark of the Covenant to Jerusalem, set it under an open tent and established over 8,000 paid singers, musicians and gatekeepers to minister to God in maintaining the worship sanctuary. *This sanctuary of unceasing worship and prayer continued day and night for 33 years.* This divine pattern of praise and petition is called the Tabernacle of David! *The Tabernacle of David is much more than just worship around the ark of God; it is the resting place of God and the center of God's governmental authority in the earth.*

The Tabernacle of David was the beginning of the reality of Heaven becoming established on the earth, as Jesus taught us to pray in the sermon on the mount (Matthew 6:10). The bringing down of Heaven to the earth begins with replicating the order and atmosphere around the central point of Heaven - the throne of God. What we observe whenever we get a glimpse of Heaven in the Bible is God seated on His throne with unceasing worship and adoration by the angels, seraphim, and elders. Everything revolves around the throne and the One seated on it! This scene around the Throne is the penultimate of worship that God desires and deserves as He is the One that created this order to meet His desires. The heavenly pattern replicated by the Tabernacle of David was established on the earth for 33 years as a foreshadowing of what is to come in the Millennial age when Jesus the High Priest sits on the throne of God in Jerusalem and begins to rule the earth from the Prayer Room (Zechariah 6:12-13).

GOD'S GOVERNMENTAL CENTER

[12]"Then say to him, 'Thus says the LORD of hosts, "Behold, a man whose name is Branch, for He will branch out from where He is; and He will build the temple of the LORD. [13]"Yes, it is He who will build the temple of the LORD, and He who will bear the honor and sit and rule on His throne. Thus, He will be a priest on His throne, and the counsel of peace will be between the two offices."' (Zechariah 6:12-13)

When King David conquered Zion, he brought the ark of God there and placed it under the tent that he pitched. It was not just a religious center that David created. He moved his entire capital city and the royal court from Gibeah, where the previous king had reigned from, to Jerusalem. David understood that the anointing for governing, both religious and civil, came from the place of the presence of God cultivated in the prayer room. He was the first to unleash the power of government from the position of prayer! This is how God's government operates - through anointed intercession.

Jesus, the One whom the government of God rests on His shoulders (Isaiah 9:6-7) is at the same time the Eternal Intercessor (Hebrews 7:25)! By creating the Tabernacle of David, the heavenly pattern of God's governmental reign was established from the place of presence, worship, and prayer. For 33 years, David kept the worship sanctuary going as he defeated the enemies of Israel and brought forth the glory of God into the earth.

The blessing and authority of the nation of Israel were directly connected to the operation of the Tabernacle of David. When Davidic worship (worship with musicians and singers) was paramount at the capital, God's blessing was on the nation. Whenever the country went away from keeping the worship sanctuary in Jerusalem, the people fell into compromise and became vulnerable. Understanding this correlation is significant if we are to operate in the fullness of God's blessing and authority as a priestly people. In our day, we want to establish God's ways as a people, not just individually, so that favor and blessings would overtake us and actively support us (2 Chronicles 16:9).

In Israel's history, there are six different seasons of revival and renewal that came after the golden years of King David and his son Solomon. In each of these revival seasons, God raised up a righteous king or leader that would seek the Lord and begin to establish His ways by reinstituting Davidic-like worship to the capital. The pattern of these six revivals of the Tabernacle of David speaks volumes to us in our day as we contend for revival and awakening in our nation and the nations of the earth!

SIX REVIVALS OF DAVIDIC WORSHIP
(worship as in the Tabernacle of David)

1) Hezekiah (2 Chronicles 29:25-27)

2) Josiah (2 Chronicles 35:3-15)

3) Zerubbabel (Ezra 3:10)

4) Ezra and Nehemiah (Nehemiah 12:24, 45)

5) Jehoiada (2 Chronicles 23:16-18)

6) Jehoshaphat (2 Chr. 20:19-28)

KINGS AND PRIESTS

and He has made us to be a kingdom, priests to His God and Father—to Him be the glory and the dominion forever and ever. Amen. (Revelation 1:6)

⁹And they sang a new song, saying, "Worthy are You to take the ₗbook and to break its seals; for You were slain, and purchased for God with Your blood men from every tribe and tongue and people and nation. ¹⁰"You have made them to be a kingdom and priests to our God; and they will reign upon the earth." (Revelation 5:9-10)

David walked in the identity of being a king *and a priest* at the same time, which was against God's rules for Israel. Israel had three primary offices in their leadership - priest, prophet and king and these three did not intermingle. King Saul impatiently offered the burnt offering in 1 Samuel 13:9 in fear of the Philistines and the people scattering. His consequence for not keeping the command of the Lord was to have his kingdom given to another man, David (1 Samuel 13). This is how grave it was for kings to violate this law and operate in the role of a priest. David could enter into this role because he identified himself with the priesthood of Melchizedek. I believe that Adam and Melchizedek both identified and operated as a king-priest way before David. Jesus is the ultimate King of Kings and High Priest-in-one who was to come. Now Jesus will walk in both these roles in the Millennial Kingdom as He will be a priest who sits on the throne in Jerusalem. The awesome part of our salvation is that we do not have to wait for the Millennial Kingdom to begin to operate as kings and priests, Jesus has made us this in Himself now through the cross! He has built us into a royal priesthood (1 Peter 2:9). *Jesus has given us the power and the access to minister to God both as a priest and with kingly authority.*

Walking in our identity as a king and priest is how God's government is established and enlarged in the earth.

THE APOSTLES PRIORITIZED MINISTRY TO GOD

"But we will devote ourselves to prayer and to the ministry of the word." (Acts 6:4)

While they were ministering to the Lord and fasting, the Holy Spirit said, "Set apart for Me Barnabas and Saul for the work to which I have called them." (Acts 13:2)

The New Testament apostles lived with a paradigm of the value of the ministry to the Lord. This is evident in the culture and communities that were created in Jerusalem in Acts 6 and then again at Antioch in Acts 13. They prioritized and centralized ministry to the Lord in worship, prayer and studying the Word so much so that they raised up other men to serve the food to release their time. As leaders of the New Testament Church, their focus was on serving and hearing God to create a healthy environment to help people. When leaders and forerunners value ministry to the Lord as central to the Church, an atmosphere is fashioned where the Holy Spirit is welcome. *This is the environment where the Lord speaks, raises up leaders and releases divine assignments to His people.*

As forerunners and priests, we must prioritize and integrate ministering to the Lord in our lives both privately and corporately. Applying this personally, at its most fundamental level, ministering to the Lord is intentionally being attentive to Him where our spirits are sensitive to what God is doing and saying. It is setting our focus, our minds, our emotions and our strength upon Him. In the natural, you can equate it to hired servants who stand ready to serve the desires of the king. So in the spirit, it is the same way. There are different ways we can understand God's wishes. Sometimes it looks like waiting on the Lord or lingering in His presence. This is strictly aligned with prayer and speaking well of God or declaring truths about God. Another way to proclaim truths of God's nature is through praise and worship where we tell God who He is. Nothing can replace the sweetness of personal devotional worship of just proclaiming to the Lord who He is! Other times, it is meeting Him in the scriptures where we learn of His mind as revealed in the Word of God. Many times as we learn of God's desires in the written Word, He begins to speak to us of His *rhema* Word. The *rhema* Word is the prophetic word that God is highlighting or the "now" Word of God for us.

Personally ministering to the Lord fuels the corporate expression when we come together. This is just as vital since God has called us to live in community. Corporate times of ministering to the Lord as a body of priests involve corporate worship and prayer, waiting on the Lord, fellowship and having communion together. I believe even times of teaching and learning can be included. As you read this, you are probably thinking this sounds like a church! Yes, that's right! I believe that *the Book of Acts expression of the church was established to minister to the Lord corporately and carry out the mission of God's redemptive story.*

When we remember that Jesus called His house a house of prayer (Matthew 21:13), and we look at how the early Church operated (Acts 2:42-47), we see the different elements included in corporately ministering to the Lord. *"They were continually devoting themselves to the apostles' teaching and to fellowship, to the breaking of bread and to prayer"* (Acts 2:42). The corporate flow and pattern of life for the local church, daily and weekly, revolved around ministering to the Lord. This is why they had daily prayer meetings, eating meals together, breaking bread from house to house and sharing in the goodness of God together. This doesn't mean that no one had a job, and everyone was at the house of prayer, but it does show that people prioritized the corporate expression of the church and came together when their schedules allowed for it, most likely daily. This idea goes against the individual nature of our lives in the West. I believe there is a shift underway that will change the expression and understanding of Christianity (how we do church) in our generation to more closely resemble the book of Acts. The Lord will unite His Church to gather around the altar and ministering to the Lord like in the days of Acts as we enter and operate in our royal priesthood.

JOHN, A PROPHETIC PATTERN

*"He who has the bride is the bridegroom; but the
friend of the bridegroom, who stands and hears him,
rejoices greatly because of the bridegroom's voice. So
this joy of mine has been made full. (John 3:29)*

The Lord sovereignly chose John the Baptist and simultaneously invited him into the place of intimacy to minister before Him in the wilderness. John accepted and entered into this privileged identity of being a friend of the bridegroom where his joy was to stand or minister to the Lord. The idea of "standing" before the Lord is symbolic in the Old Testament, used to describe someone ministering to the Lord. The prototypical forerunner lived this type of lifestyle as a priest that would release the anointing to prepare Israel for the first coming of Jesus. We observe from John's life that fundamental or innate to the forerunner calling is living in our priestly identity. Forerunners must learn how to minister to God because it is while ministering to the Lord that we can receive from God (John 3:27). John was more than a phenomenon, his lifestyle, ministry, and message is a prophetic pattern given to the Body of Christ on how to prepare the Earth for Jesus' second coming. *In seeing this pattern, we must give ourselves to this type of lifestyle to develop and hone our hearts, gifts, and message to be a clear voice in our generation!*

KEY UNDERSTANDING

The forerunner ministry is founded and rooted in the priesthood. The calculated way in which God announced John's birth and forerunner calling is a sign to us of the significance of ministering to the Lord. End-time forerunners, following the pattern laid out by John, will call the Body of Christ back to the foundation of the priestly identity and service. The corporate dimension of ministry to the Lord is revealed in the context of God's house, the House of Prayer. God will fill the earth with a global incense arising from the priesthood of all believers to create the context for the return of Christ.

A PRAYER FOR FORERUNNERS

Dear Heavenly Father,

I pray for the revelation of the significance of the priesthood to shape the forerunners that You are preparing in our day. Help us to understand the privilege You have given to us as those who are called kings and priests before Your throne. I pray that we would walk in the nearness of having access to Your heart and the authority of bringing forth Your Kingdom.

Lord, impart in every forerunner the sense of priority of ministering to the Lord all the days of their lives both privately and corporately. May we never stray away from gazing in wonder at our King. Captivate our hearts and bring back wonder again as we behold the King of glory.

In the matchless name of Jesus,

AMEN!

CHAPTER 7

GOD'S ZEAL FOR THE HOUSE OF PRAYER

My House Shall be Called a House of Prayer

THE END-TIME PRAYER MOVEMENT

*"For from the rising of the sun even to its setting, My
name will be great among the nations, and in every
place incense is going to be offered to My name, and
a grain offering that is pure; for My name will
be great among the nations," says the LORD of hosts.
(Malachi 1:11)*

It is no coincidence or mistake that the prayer movement is
exploding throughout the earth as God is raising up
forerunners at the end of the age. The Body of Christ will
again operate in her true identity as the royal priesthood,
praying in unity which ushered in Pentecost (Acts 2). This

time, however, there will be a global incense movement from every nation that will prepare the earth for a worldwide Pentecost called "the outpouring of the Holy Spirit" that will precede the second coming of Christ. John's life was a prophetic pattern revealing to end-time forerunners how to operate in this priestly identity and steward the global worship and prayer movement. The global Church operating as The House of Prayer (Matthew 21:13) will set the context for the people of God to walk in maturity and purity, overcome persecution and the Antichrist system, and to partner with the Lord in bringing in the Great Harvest of souls from every nation. The incense from the worldwide House of Prayer movement will produce a global "upper room" in preparation for the full release of the Joel 2 outpouring of the Spirit!

"On that day I will raise up the tabernacle of David, which has fallen down, and repair its damages; I will raise up its ruins, and rebuild it as in the days of old;
(Amos 9:11)

Amos received the original prophetic declaration that the Tabernacle of David would be rebuilt and re-established at the end of the age. After comparing Amos 9 with its quote in Acts 15 at the Council of Jerusalem, I believe the physical Tabernacle of David will be rebuilt by Jesus in Jerusalem after He returns. However, *in the last generation that ushers in the return of Christ, Israel is restored to their land after their dispersion, and the spirit of the Tabernacle of David will be released in ever increasing measure to build the house of prayer for all nations!*

THE PURPOSE OF NIGHT AND DAY PRAYER

The establishment of the House of Prayer movement in the spirit of the Tabernacle of David is at the forefront of God's prophetic strategy in converging all the significant moves of God to prepare for the return of Christ. This is a bold statement, but one I believe is validated from the scriptures below as we look at the strategic placement of night and day prayer. In other words, the establishment of night and day prayer is the glue or the foundation upon which God will fulfill all the mandates of redemptive history.

Here is a brief sketch of night and day prayer involved in the end-time move of God.

1) **Declaration of the Worthiness of Jesus**: Night and day worship and prayer is first and foremost for Jesus' sake. We declare that He is worthy above all else. It is our expression of first love (Matthew 22:37) as God restores the First Commandment to first place.

    ... saying with a loud voice, "Worthy is the Lamb that was slain to receive power and riches and wisdom and might and honor and glory and blessing." (Revelation 5:12)

2) **The Building of the Church**: God's House is to be identified as a House of Prayer. As she walks in this identity, He will build His Church/House once again. The raising up of the House of Prayer movement is to help build the Church.

And He began to teach and say to them, "Is it not written, 'My house shall be called a house of prayer for all the nations'? But you have made it a robbers den." (Mark 11:17)

⁶"Also the foreigners who join themselves to the LORD, to minister to Him, and to love the name of the LORD, to be His servants, everyone who keeps from profaning the Sabbath and holds fast My covenant; ⁷Even those I will bring to My holy mountain and make them joyful in My house of prayer. Their burnt offerings and their sacrifices will be acceptable on My altar; For My house will be called a house of prayer for all the peoples." ⁸The Lord GOD, who gathers the dispersed of Israel, declares, "Yet others I will gather to them, to those already gathered." (Isaiah 56:6-8)

I also say to you that you are Peter, and upon this rock I will build My church, and the gates of Hades will not overpower it. (Matthew 16:18)

3) **The Purposes of Israel**: God has promised to set watchmen on the walls for Jerusalem's sake until she is made a praise in the earth. These watchmen operate in the spirit of the Tabernacle of David; they will pray until all of Israel is saved and Jesus returns to deliver Jerusalem.

⁶On your walls, O Jerusalem, I have appointed watchmen; All day and all night they will never keep silent. You who remind the LORD, take no rest for yourselves; ⁷And give Him no rest until He establishes and makes Jerusalem a praise in the earth. (Isaiah 62:6-7)

4) **The Release of Justice:** We pray for justice in mercy—the release of God's ways in government and society.

⁵In mercy the throne will be established; and One will sit on it in truth, in the tabernacle of David, judging and seeking justice and hastening righteousness. (Isaiah 16:5)

Now, will not God bring about justice for His elect who cry to Him day and night, and will He delay long over them? (Luke 18:7)

5) **The Harvest:** One of the major applications in the Scripture of the restoration of David's Tabernacle was related to the salvation of the Gentiles-- the "rest of mankind."

¹⁶'After these things, I will return and will rebuild the tabernacle of David which has fallen, and I will rebuild its ruins, and I will restore it, ¹⁷So that the rest of mankind may seek the LORD, even all the Gentiles who are called by My name." (Acts 15:16-17)

[37]Then He said to His disciples, "The harvest truly is plentiful, but the laborers are few. [38]"Therefore pray the Lord of the harvest to send out laborers into His harvest." (Matthew 9:37-38)

6) **The Salvation of the Arabs:** One result of the tabernacle of David is that Jesus may possess the remnant of Edom. Edom speaks of the Arab nations, especially the Islamic ones. Therefore, *a key to overcoming Islam is for the Church to function in night and day prayer.*

[11]"In that day I will raise up the fallen booth of David, and wall up its breaches; I will also raise up its ruins and rebuild it as in the days of old; [12]That they may possess the remnant of Edom and all the nations who are called by My name," declares the LORD who does this. (Amos 9:11-12)

RE-ENVISIONED TO BUILD THE HOUSE OF PRAYER

My wife and I followed the House of Prayer movement, however, during our wilderness years we were not actively involved. We attended some conferences in Kansas City, kept in contact with friends and leaders, and had a distant pulse on what was happening but didn't jump back in until the IHOPU Awakening. A small group of friends attended the annual Onething Conference in December 2009 when the student awakening was taking place. During the first session of the conference, I began to weep. My heart felt the witness of the

Holy Spirit and the Lord was recasting vision in me to build the House of Prayer in Sarasota! As we left Kansas City that year, I knew the Lord was transitioning my family and me; however, I didn't know where we were going!

Transition seasons hold unique, intriguing circumstances and situations that only the Lord can bring together. I learned that transitions could take years, not weeks or months as most expect. God begins to increase the desire in our hearts for what He has so that we will pursue Him with greater fervor. Also, He fuels that desire with a higher activity of the Holy Spirit. In many ways, transition seasons are like divine scavenger hunts gathering and fitting together the puzzle pieces that God has given in the past with fresh prophetic encounters, words, and understanding. Indeed, it is God's way of inviting us into His story while writing our prophetic journey. Looking back, I see God's wisdom and faithfulness as He meticulously worked in the details while He led us.

To fast forward our story, 2011 to 2013 was a divine season of grace as Jennifer and I began to walk publicly in what God was calling us to do. It started with an idea to host a monthly, youth prayer-rally for revival in our city. We worked with churches on prayer initiatives for the ending of violence in Newtown (our inner city), and the Lord began to connect me with pastors and leaders to strengthen prayer in our region. Simultaneously, I entered into a season of extended fasting for a breakthrough. During this two-year time frame, by the grace of God, I did three 40-day water fasts and in between them, two 21-day water fasts. I had fasted before but never like this or for this length of time. I began to see God move in miraculous ways as I stepped into His invitation.

I do not usually reveal my fasting. I am sharing this with you, my readers, to understand what may be asked or required of you to press through to all the Lord desires. It is only by His grace and invitation that this can be accomplished.

FASTING PREPARES THE WAY

"For John came neither eating nor drinking, and they say, 'He has a demon!' (Matthew 11:18)

Let me add a side note on fasting as there seems to be much fear and confusion on this subject. Fasting does not "earn" anything from God. It doesn't give us more favor, solidify our calling or put us on God's good side. If we fast to gain more approval from God, we are doing it with a wrong motivation and a wrong spirit. God always gives generously with purity from a place of grace and the abundance of His heart and nature. Then you may ask, "Why fast?"

Fasting has so many spiritual benefits that many are unaware of and miss out on. Simply put, *fasting prepares our hearts to be able to receive MORE from God and in a faster manner.* There are three primary benefits of fasting: It strengthens our spiritual man, enlarges our hearts to receive more, and accelerates our ability to partner with the Lord. In fasting, we deny our God-given appetite for the basic necessity of food to focus on the Lord, who in turn strengthens our spiritual man. Essentially, when we begin our fast, we are declaring that our love and need for God is greater than our own desires and self-love. We strengthen our inner man while putting to death the desires of our flesh; as Paul says in Romans 6:14, "***sin shall not be master over you.***"

Fasting also sensitizes our spirit to God and increases our capacity to receive and hold more from God. It is what Isaiah described in chapter 54 when he said to "enlarge the place of your tent; stretch out the curtains of your dwellings." I believe there is much that God wants to give us but we are unable to receive or hold the revelation, anointing, and favor due to the smallness of our hearts. *Fasting is a spiritual discipline given by God to partner with Him to grow our hearts.*

As our spirits grow more sensitive to the Holy Spirit, we can submit and agree with what God is doing more easily and quickly. This agreement accelerates our partnership with God in receiving revelation and allows His plans to be established faster.

John the Baptist had a lifestyle of fasting in the wilderness. It was part of his preparation as well as his lifestyle as he ministered. Jesus affirms this in Matthew 11 as He spoke to the crowds about John's life and ministry. It is my conviction that *every forerunner needs to live a lifestyle that includes regular fasting.* The early church did-- they fasted two days a week! It is vital to keep our spirits strong, our hearts humble, to receive fresh revelation from the Lord, and to partner with Him to build the Kingdom.

GOD IS SPEAKING

Let me share with you one experience that happened during my first 40-day fast. I had finished ministering at a Russian Church in town and was getting ready to leave when an elderly Ukrainian lady came running to my car. She was holding a packet in her hand and kept saying in broken English, "For you! For you!" I turned over the packet and instantly knew what I was holding. Hurriedly, I searched for anyone that could speak Ukrainian. I wanted to know how she got this paper and why she was giving it to me. After talking through an interpreter, I learned she felt the Lord had told her to give this paper to me but still, to this day, I don't know where she got it from. The packet she handed me was a pristine, new copy of a prophetic warning my pastor had written in 1992 called "God is Speaking." In it, he urged the Church to repent and prepare as impending judgment was coming to our region! He had predicted a hurricane would come and boldly broadcasted the news throughout our area with a handwritten, short treatise. The storm never occurred; however, the prediction brought a lot of turmoil to our little congregation. I believe the underlying premise for the need of the Church to repent and be cleansed was correct, and that a time of unprecedented difficulties and judgment is yet coming to the nations. This paper had much significance to our fellowship and in our prophetic journey. She brought it to me seemingly out of nowhere after 20 years, and God was undeniably speaking to us! This began a series of miraculous God-initiated events, and we knew the Lord was leading us.

CONSECRATE

In the fall of 2012, I met with John and Michelle Skorski, a couple who runs a ministry called "The Front" in Bradenton. As we were discussing how we can collaborate to minister to the youth and young adults in our region, we decided to hold a youth and young adult conference together in June right after school let out. I had never run a conference or an event nor was I even in full-time ministry. But I had the vision to mobilize and unite the Church in our region in prayer for our young people! Specifically, I wanted to hold 40 days of prayer leading up to the conference with 40 churches opening their doors to contend for this generation in prayer. Also, I wanted to do this simultaneously in the tri-city region of Sarasota, Bradenton, and Venice. So we began targeting three cities and forty churches in each city to host one prayer meeting before our youth conference. On top of all that, I wanted to offer the whole event for free just like they did at Onething at IHOPKC. This was no small task!

As we began our journey, the Lord woke me up early one morning and gave me the verse out of Jeremiah 1:5, *"**Before I formed you in the womb I knew you, and before you were born I consecrated you; I have appointed you a prophet to the nations.**"* From this verse, the Consecrate youth and young adult conference was birthed! Our primary theme for Consecrate was calling a generation to live in holiness and become empowered by the love of God. The Lord gave us a three-fold mandate for this young generation: **Created - Called - Commissioned.** He wanted us to declare to this broken generation that they were not a mistake but *Created* for destiny in the love of God, *Called* to be radical followers of Jesus Christ and *Commissioned* for the Gospel by the Holy Spirit. This has been our rallying cry over our children as we contend for their futures!

I had a small home transcription business when we launched out in preparing for Consecrate. I hired and trained a part-time employee to take over my work so I could be set free. For the next six months I gave myself to this conference. I did three rounds of meetings. First, I met with senior pastors to share the vision of Consecrate, get their "blessing" to host a night of prayer at their church and ask for them to sow in financially for our youth. Second, the next round of meetings was with youth pastors so that they would organize and rally their teens to come to Consecrate. Third, the final and most challenging set of meetings was with business people and individuals whom I asked to fund the event.

In total, we had 110 churches over three cities that hosted nights of prayer over the 40 days leading up to Consecrate! We had so many nationalities and denominations that joined in- from Hispanic and black churches to Korean, Brazilian and Ukrainian congregations. Some were conservative, others full gospel and charismatic. We prayed with all styles of worship and praise as well- ultraconservative denominations where instruments were not used, to gospel worship to contemporary worship. It didn't matter to our little team; we got to meet and pray with all different kinds of brothers and sisters in Christ night after night for 40 days, sometimes twice a day. I believe the angels were smiling as it must have looked like a slice of heaven on earth seeing the Church pray together in unity. We have done 40 days of prayer in various ways each year as we prepare for Consecrate. As my wife said, "I don't ever want to imagine what Consecrate would look like if we didn't pray!"

As I look back on those days, the favor and grace of God were so prevalent as He gave me a clear survey of the Christian landscape in our region. I made many pastoral and marketplace friends during this time. It was as if God gave me an accelerated class on how churches operated and an inside peek into their hearts. What I didn't realize was that through these relationships God was setting the stage to build the House of Prayer in Sarasota!

A MIRACULOUS BUILDING

During mid-March of 2013, right in the midst of preparing for Consecrate and the 40 Days of Prayer, I received a call from a gentleman with a family estate. He wanted to show me a building on the edge of Newtown that had previously been used for a homeless ministry. A local church had purchased the land, cleared it and invested 1.2 million dollars in building it in 2006. Unfortunately, the ministry had gone bankrupt by 2011, and there was a fence around the property as we drove up. Taking the tour and walking through the commercial kitchen where they fed over 1000 people a week, the computer lab, the showers, and laundry facility and the various rooms, I couldn't figure out how we would use it. Finally he asked me, "Can you do a house of prayer here?" My astute discerning answer was "No!" We were praying and looking for a building to start a house of prayer but this building had no prayer room, was built for outreach and to minister to the homeless. I couldn't see it.

On a Wednesday night six weeks later, while at home, I somehow internally could "see" how we could use the homeless ministry building for a house of prayer. The next day I received a random invitation from a pastor acquaintance to attend some meetings he was having with a Nigerian apostle beginning that night. My wife and I went to the meeting and that Nigerian pastor preached the last six months of my life. We then went to every meeting he had that weekend, and the Lord gave me three confirmations over the weekend about the house of prayer.

On Monday morning I called the gentleman with the family estate and asked to revisit the fenced-up building again. By the end of the week, the family with the estate put an offer on the property. Over the ensuing weeks, the family with the estate went back and forth with the bank negotiating in an attempt to settle on the accurate appraisal price of the building. In June, a Russian man who didn't speak English was praying for our building and received a vision of us. He saw a train pull up and the doors opened. We then had a decision to make, either we could get on the train or the doors would close and the train would pass us by. However, if we got on the train, he said we would be running and still barely keeping up with what God would do. After receiving the vision from this Russian man I called the estate and urged them to make the highest offer possible. Time was beginning to run out and we didn't want the train to pass us by!

THE SARASOTA HOUSE OF PRAYER

In mid-June 2013 we held our first Consecrate conference. Wow! It had blown up on us. We had over 1200 students who came for three days to encounter Jesus from over 150 churches! It was an incredible three days which we will never forget. I got a call on the Friday morning after Consecrate from my best friend, Jim Good, who was brokering the deal for the building. He said, "Guess what you are going to be doing for the next ten years?" I had no idea. We had just finished an impossible dream with Consecrate! What was next? He went on, "You are going to be running a House of Prayer!" The bank had accepted the offer on the building. The surprising part was the family with the estate didn't give their best offer but instead had made a lower bid. We closed on the building on August 15, 2013, renovated it as best we could and opened the Sarasota House of Prayer on October 1, 2013, going 40 hours a week! It was a dream come true for Jennifer and me!

We are now almost five years into maintaining the altar of the Lord in the prayer room at the Sarasota House of Prayer; we have watched the Lord build the house of prayer. There is a thriving young adult community operating in their priestly identity, ministering to the Lord and contending for revival in the prayer room. Over the past five years, the Lord has brought leaders and full-time staff, opened a full-time ministry school and worship school, offered multiple internships, created outreach initiatives and so much more. And I believe we have only just begun to touch the surface of what God desires to create here in this region!

GOD'S DREAM

On that day I will raise up the Tabernacle of David, which has fallen down, and repair its damages; I will raise up its ruins, and rebuild it as in the days of old; (Amos 9:11)

Over the past five years, I have begun to understand the sovereign nature of God raising up the global prayer movement. When Jennifer and I started, we said "yes" to the invitation of God thinking we wanted to build a prayer room in Sarasota. Little did I know that it is God's desire to build the House of Prayer first and foremost and that He will supply everything necessary. I share our story of God's direction and grace to encourage you and strengthen you in the journey and share with you what God wants to do firsthand. As I look back over the past five years at the Sarasota House of Prayer and the last twenty years since I left Kansas City, I see God's faithfulness in spite of my struggles and weaknesses. The global prayer movement and the House of Prayer is truly God's idea and divine, prophetic pattern. The hardest part of our job is to be able to "see" it and remain in His path as He builds the House of Prayer in the nations.

The global prayer movement, which has grown exponentially in the past 20 years around the nations, is the Bride of Christ rising to our priestly identity and responding to the dream of God's heart. The people of God around the world are beginning to grab hold of the prophetic declaration that the Lord will one day cover the earth with worship and incense day and night. There is an alignment happening in our day to where we are positioning ourselves to prioritize ministering to God *first,* which births all other service unto God. Amos prophesied about a coming day when the restoration and fullness of the Tabernacle of David will fill the entire earth-- which is night and day worship and prayer led by Jesus ruling from Jerusalem!

KEY UNDERSTANDING

In God's divine strategy and pattern, He is using night and day prayer in the context of the House of Prayer as the point of the arrow to fulfill His redemptive plan in the earth. As I have expounded in this chapter, night and day prayer is foundational to every major movement that God is culminating at the end of the age! For this reason, we have to understand why and how God is sovereignly raising up the house of prayer movement all through the nations in our generation: it's so that we can partner with Him!

A PRAYER FOR FORERUNNERS

Dear Heavenly Father,

Thank You for raising up the House of Prayer in the nations of the earth! I pray that You would establish Your heavenly pattern of night and day worship and prayer all over the globe in our generation. Mark every forerunner with the vision and cry of Psalm 132 to see the dwelling place of God set in the earth. Give them a resolve, like David, to build the house of prayer for all nations in the cities that You have placed them in. Release divine unction and anointing to carry Your burden to establish a culture of prayer in the people of God.

Lord, let the prayer rooms throughout the world become birthing chambers of divine (spiritual) understanding and assignments. Send out Your forerunners, prepared from these prayer rooms, as arrows of light into the nations and our culture.

In the mighty name of Jesus!

AMEN!

CHAPTER 8

COMFORTING ISRAEL

Having God's Heart for Israel

MY REVELATION OF ISRAEL

Jennifer and I would sit and talk in the trailer-office during our internship at Master's Commission and "solve" all the problems of the Church! While discussing the many issues of our day, she would regularly bring up the topic of Israel and the Jewish people. At that time, I had no understanding or grid for Israel. I had read about the Jews in the Bible but had no other reference point; I hadn't even seen the eccentric shofar-blowing men or the flag-waving women at conferences yet. I was just plain ignorant, yet Jennifer kept bringing up this topic to me.

In May of 1999, I had a month of divine revelation. Many of the topics the Lord gave to me were in seed form. It was as if the DNA was given to me back then, and I have since been on a journey studying, sharing and living out these truths. For my wife and I, they have become the foundational values and messages that we have carried. One of these divine revelations was the importance of God's heart for Israel.

I had been hearing about the Great Harvest of Souls that was coming, and that people were praying for this from different camps and movements. It was a relatively easy topic or assignment to rally around and work together for in unity in the Body of Christ. The Great Harvest seemed to supersede differing end-time views, or other controversial positions as the focus on the souls of men prevailed. As I pursued this more in-depth, I suddenly had the realization that central to the Great Harvest and End-Time preparation was the position and role of the nation of Israel. I could "see" the Great Harvest and End-Times spiraling together like the two stands in the double helix model that make up our DNA. Different nitrogen bases pair together in the middle to create the core of the DNA. I understood the two strands were the Great Harvest and the End-Times with Israel being the core, which is the driving force. So without Israel in the picture, you could not have the Great Harvest and End-Time events in their right place. This DNA illustration isn't a perfect picture, but from my biology background, it made sense in my mind. God is amazingly personal in that He knows how to speak our language so we can understand Him!

JOHN SENT TO CONFRONT ISRAEL

¹⁶And he will turn many of the sons of Israel back to the Lord their God...¹⁷so as to make ready a people prepared for the Lord." (Luke 1:16-17)

John the Baptist, the preeminent and prototypical forerunner in the Scriptures, was commissioned to *"make ready a people prepared for the Lord* (Luke 1:17)." His life was both a message in itself but also an arrow that was shot into the nation. John was to prepare the Lord's way by getting the people of Israel ready for the Messiah who was to come. The turning of the hearts of the sons of Israel was part of the preparatory work that was necessary to create the environment for the Lord to come. Underlying this commission was the Lord's view of Israel, that they were walking in disobedience and not ready to receive the promises of God. John's preaching of repentance to Israel was a confrontation sent by God.

⁸"Therefore bear fruit in keeping with repentance; ⁹and do not suppose that you can say to yourselves, 'We have Abraham for our father'; for I say to you that from these stones God is able to raise up children to Abraham." (Matthew 3:8-9)

God was challenging and waking up the slumbering nation through John's anointed preaching. The call to repentance was an offensive view to the Jews who considered themselves chosen and blessed of God inherently because they were

Abraham's physical offspring. For generations they held onto a false presupposition that they were in good standing with God and ready to receive the Kingdom of God. John's message was a sword to the paradigm of their religious culture and was sent to expose the carnality of their hearts.

ISRAEL IS NOT FORSAKEN

For the LORD your God in the midst of you is a jealous God; otherwise, the anger of the LORD your God will be kindled against you (Deuteronomy 6:15)

What John was revealing through his confrontational preaching was that Israel, as a nation, had a much larger problem than the Roman occupation and oppression; they had to deal with the God of Israel! Yahweh had chosen, called and made a covenant with Israel - one that He will not break. Through Israel's history, He revealed Himself as a jealous God in their midst with great emotions of love, so much so that He compared His relationship with Israel to a bridegroom with His bride (Isaiah 54:5-6). The gloriously difficult issue for Israel is that God is after her whole undivided heart to Him, and He will not let her go when she disobeys. Instead, God's nature is to actually draw closer and intervene more intimately through discipline to get Israel's attention. He will do whatever it takes as a jealous lover to capture Israel's wholehearted love and devotion. God will pursue Israel until the end of the age to win her heart! This pursuit of God after His people Israel sets the context for the end-time events.

Without understanding God's commitment to Israel, the end-time events of the Bible leading to the Day of the Lord will not make sense.

I say then, they did not stumble so as to fall, did they? May it never be! But by their transgression salvation has come to the Gentiles, to make them jealous. (Romans 11:11)

Paul makes it abundantly clear in Romans 9-11, his masterpiece treatise on Israel's central role in the redemptive storyline of God, that Israel has not been forsaken permanently by God. Though they have stumbled in sin and unbelief individually, as a corporate people God's election has not been removed from them. They are still under the election of God, or in a relationship with the covenant-keeping God. Israel's election is firm in the New Testament. But what's more surprising is the role that the Gentile Church is given in Israel's salvation plan.

Israel's transgression or rejection of Messiah, which is an enormous negative in the flesh, brought forth salvation to the Gentiles in God's plan. However, the Lord gave this salvation with a purpose-- to provoke Israel to jealousy so that they will come back to the Lord their God. He has given the Gentile Church throughout the nations an immense responsibility. The totality of the Church's fruit and actions must lead to the provocation of the nation of Israel. Humbly, Israel's regathering and salvation does not depend solely on Israel nor are they able to fulfill their own calling for their people. Now they must rely on the maturity and service of the Gentile Church, as much as they might not like this, for Israel to experience their full salvation and calling. To think that the family through which the Gospel came (Romans 1:16; 9:5) now needs to have the Gospel sent to them by the Gentiles. It's an incredible plan only God could have come up with to bring unity and humility to all peoples (Romans 11:32-33)!

THE MYSTERY OF ISRAEL

25 For I do not want you, brethren, to be uninformed of this mystery—so that you will not be wise in your own estimation—that a partial hardening has happened to Israel until the fullness of the Gentiles has come in; 26 and so all Israel will be saved; just as it is written, "The deliverer will come from Zion; he will remove ungodliness from Jacob."
(Romans 11:25-26)

Paul includes the Gentiles in what he calls the Mystery of Israel. There is a significant role that the Gentiles play in this mysterious and unexpected storyline of Israel's redemption. God has placed a partial hardening on the people of Israel until the fullness of the Gentiles has come in. In other words, this partial hardening will not be completely lifted until two things take place: 1) The full number of Gentiles comes into the Kingdom of God, and 2) The Gentile Church walks in her full maturity. Due to Israel's rejection of Jesus the Messiah, God has placed this contingency on her salvation. The fullness of the Gentiles must come to pass first so that she may receive her full salvation along with the Gentiles; thus, walking in the One New Man reality that Paul described in Ephesians 2:15.

Let me mention a couple of things here on the partial hardening or blindness that is upon Israel. First, it is partial, meaning that not all Jews are hardened or blinded. That means that there are some Jews that do believe in Jesus and receive Him as Savior. This remnant has been present from the first century and has actually increased exponentially in the past 100 years as the Messianic movement has come forth. Second, the hardening is temporary. It will lift when the fullness of the Gentiles come into the Kingdom of God. A time is coming when the blindness will lift off of Israel, and they will be able to see Jesus for who He really is. This will happen in conjunction with the outpouring of the Spirit of grace and supplication (Zechariah 12:10) on the house of David while they are being surrounded by the nations (Zechariah 12:3; 14:2) before Jesus delivers them. We need to remember the end-time context that Israel finds herself in before the partial hardening is removed, she is delivered, and thus "all Israel is saved!" This period is part of the baptism of fire that John was preaching long ago in the first century.

"As for me, I baptize you with water for repentance, but He who is coming after me is mightier than I, and I am not fit to remove His sandals; He will baptize you with the Holy Spirit and fire. (Matthew 3:11)

John's message of repentance and his revelation of the One who was coming to baptize with the Holy Spirit and fire was not an isolated idea. Israel in the Old Testament understood the eschatological or end-time punishments on Israel and the nations. The baptism of fire is not a foreign concept but would have been recognized by the first century Jews as God bringing His judgment or fire upon everything that resists God, including Israel. When John said that the Messiah would baptize with the Holy Spirit and fire, he was ultimately speaking of the judgment that would come at the end of the age. He was addressing the last generation before the return of Christ. We know this because the baptism of the Holy Spirit was fulfilled at Pentecost in Acts 3. This is the same principle that Jesus Himself revealed in Luke 4 when He took the scroll in the synagogue. He got up and began to read Isaiah 61. He read up to "the favorable year of the Lord" and then sat down. Next, He made an astounding comment in verse 21, *"Today this scripture has been fulfilled in your hearing."* What must have the people thought as their "eyes were fixed on Him!" Jesus was saying that the anointing to preach the gospel unto salvation, including the baptism of the Holy Spirit, was at hand and fulfilled in Himself. Interestingly enough, He did not read the next part of Isaiah 61:2 which reads, *"And the day of vengeance of our God."* It is because the day of vengeance, or the baptism of fire, is God's punishment and purifying fire that is released at the end of the age before the Lord's second coming.

To understand this, John was saying that the Messiah was both the Savior who poured out His Spirit at Pentecost to empower as well as the Judge who will again pour out His Spirit in the last days to purify. This is the commitment that God has made to Israel. He will not leave her alone in her sin and wanderings but will do whatever it takes to win her heart over and purify her. God will do it on a global stage in front of all the nations as He brings and allows the pressures of the Enemy and the Antichrist, through countries led by unrighteous men, and His judgments to bend Israel's knee so that they will call upon the name of Jesus. The leaders of Israel will shout "*blessed is He who comes in the name of the Lord*" (Matthew 23:39) as they welcome Jesus as their Messiah and King.

WATCHMEN ON THE WALL

⁶On your walls, O Jerusalem, I have appointed watchmen; All day and all night they will never keep silent. You who remind the LORD, take no rest for yourselves; ⁷And give Him no rest until He establishes and makes Jerusalem a praise in the earth. (Isaiah 62:6-7)

One of the primary purposes of God raising up the Church worldwide in her identity as the House of Prayer is to stand with the nation of Israel and God's redemptive plans for her. In Isaiah 62:6-7, we get a glimpse into the way the people of God will operate in that last generation. The Lord will enlist watchmen over the entire earth so that collectively in geographic regions the Church will be praying day and night for God's purposes for Israel to come to pass. This will continue until Jerusalem becomes a praise in the earth. From other parts of the Scriptures, Jerusalem will be contested until Jesus returns and the Prince of Peace Himself rules from the restored Tabernacle of David. It is to this end that God is enlisting forerunners in our day. The forerunners of this last generation will have insight with understanding (Daniel 9:22) in order to lead, direct and mobilize the Body of Christ to stand with the nation of Israel according to God's strategic timing and plan.

'Alas! for that day is great, there is none like it; And it is the time of Jacob's distress, but he will be saved from it. (Jeremiah 30:7)

"Now at that time Michael, the great prince who stands guard over the sons of your people, will arise. And there will be a time of distress such as never occurred since there was a nation until that time; and at that time your people, everyone who is found written in the book, will be rescued. (Daniel 12:1)

"For then there will be a great tribulation, such as has not occurred since the beginning of the world until now, nor ever will. (Matthew 24:21)

The forerunners who lead the Gentile Church to stand with the nation of Israel will be desperately needed. The Scriptures predict a future day when a great tribulation will come upon the Jewish people. This time frame is referred to in Jeremiah as the "time of Jacob's distress or trouble" and will last three and one-half years. The targeted persecution against the Jewish people will be worldwide and much broader in scope than the Holocaust in Germany. It is during the context of this great tribulation in which the provocation of the Jews to jealousy by the Gentiles will occur (Romans 11:11) as the Church will serve, suffer and stand with Israel until Messiah comes to deliver us all.

> [1]*"Comfort, O comfort My people," says your God.*
> [2]*"Speak kindly to Jerusalem; And call out to her, that her warfare has ended, that her iniquity has been removed, that she has received of the LORD'S hand double for all her sins."* [3]*A voice is calling, "Clear the way for the LORD in the wilderness; Make smooth in the desert a highway for our God.*
> *(Isaiah 40:1-3)*

Forerunners who enter into God's heart for Israel now will be able to comfort her in the days of difficulty that are coming. We will be trained now in the early days to love, serve and pray for Israel no matter what the cost will be. If you feel that this message of the forerunner is resonating in your hearts, it is imperative that you understand God's plan and heart for the Jewish people. I want to reiterate that Israel is not a side issue but is central to God's redemptive plan. If we would be voices and leaders in the upcoming move of God, we forerunners must pray and serve the purposes of God for Israel as part of our calling. This may not be the only assignment that the Lord gives us, but I'm sure it will be included. Now is the time to get invested in Israel and have our hearts challenged and enlarged in love so that we may accept and serve the prophetic call of the Jewish people. To love and minister to Israel, you must understand God's master plan for her. I want to strongly encourage you to study and firmly grasp Paul's arguments in Romans 9-11. These three chapters are a non-negotiable if you are to stand with God's heart for Israel.

KEY UNDERSTANDING

As forerunners, we must understand the Biblical covenants and God's overarching storyline from Genesis to Revelation. The Biblical storyline will end where it began, with Israel at the center. As we draw closer to the return of Christ, the events of the world will begin to centralize around Israel, specifically Jerusalem, both in importance and in geographic proximity. This focus is consistent with the Biblical testimony which repeats over and over of Israel's central role in the redemptive storyline and God's undeniable commitment to fulfill it! To this end, *one of the primary purposes of the forerunner ministry is to be a watchman over the nation of Israel and to serve God's purposes concerning her.*

A PRAYER FOR FORERUNNERS

Father of Glory,

We thank You and honor Your choice of the nation of Israel as Your sovereign vessel. We bless Your wisdom in leading and protecting her over the centuries. Thank You for Your unending mercies over the Jewish people and that Your calling and election over her are sure and steadfast.

In this hour, raise up those who would love and serve Your purposes for Israel. According to Your prophetic pattern, build and establish night and day prayer in the nations to partner with Your heart for the salvation and protection of the Jewish people. Raise up faithful witnesses filled with insight and understanding to mobilize the body of Christ to serve Israel.

We pray even now for the people of Israel - comfort them with the good news and the promise of hope found in the person of Christ Jesus. Send forth a Gospel witness from the Church that would provoke the Jews to jealousy and turn their hearts! Holy Spirit, come and reveal Jesus Messiah who would heal their hearts and save their families.

We pray these things in the strong name of Jesus,

Amen!

CHAPTER 9

THE SPIRIT OF ELIJAH

The Blessing of Spiritual Fathers and Mothers

SPIRIT AND POWER OF ELIJAH

"It is he who will go as a forerunner before Him in the spirit and power of Elijah, to turn the hearts of the fathers back to the children, and the disobedient to the attitude of the righteous, so as to make ready a people prepared for the Lord." (Luke 1:17)

Gabriel announced to Zacharias that John would live and minister as a forerunner in the "spirit and power of Elijah." What does this mean? Elijah was revered in Israel's history as a prophet who confronted Baal and the false prophets by fire on Mount Carmel during the reign of Ahab (1 Kings 18).

His life and ministry were marked by supernatural miracles of all sorts. He is also the one who was taken up to Heaven alive in a whirlwind as God sent a chariot with horses of fire that snatched him up (2 Kings 2:11). Elijah's protégé Elisha was there to witness this incredible event with his own two eyes as he received his master's mantle and a double portion of his anointing.

"Behold, I am going to send you Elijah the prophet before the coming of the great and terrible day of the LORD. (Malachi 4:5)

Malachi concludes the Old Testament by stating a cryptic warning that Elijah will come back in the future. His future return would precede the great and terrible Day of the Lord. This Day-of-the-Lord theme is prevalent throughout the Old Testament and refers to the day of God's ultimate victory over the nations and their judgment. The sending of Elijah in this verse is meant to be seen as God's mercy to the people before God's dealings with Israel and the nations in His judgments. God always sends mercy before judgment. From Malachi's prophetic declaration, there was built into Israel's culture, even until today, an expectancy that Elijah would return in bodily form in the future.

Just as the hope of Messiah's coming will be fulfilled in two stages or two comings, so will the arrival of Elijah be fulfilled in two separate stages. John the Baptist came as the first installment of the coming of Elijah, but there is another coming that is yet predicted, meaning there is a final Elijah who is to come. John came in the spirit and power of Elijah (Luke 1:17), but he clearly stated that he was not Elijah (John 1:21). Jesus referenced that same notion when He said that "*if you are willing to accept it, John himself is Elijah who was to come*" (Matthew 11:14). However, Jesus also said that "*Elijah is coming and will restore all things*" (Matthew 17:11). The coming of Elijah is connected to the restoration of all things; we are in desperate need of this eternal restoration which is still yet to happen. John was a down-payment of what Elijah would do but is not the final fulfillment. There is, however, a future fulfillment of Elijah's coming that must occur before the great and terrible Day of the Lord. This coming will either be physical, in bodily form, or in the spirit that Elijah carried as seen in John.

RESTORING THE HEARTS OF THE FATHERS

"He will restore the hearts of the fathers to their children and the hearts of the children to their fathers so that I will not come and smite the land with a curse." (Malachi 4:6)

Malachi goes on to describe what Elijah would do before the Day of the Lord. Interestingly, the message of mercy that God will send before the judgment of that Day is one of restoring relationships between fathers and their children! This verse is a huge statement that reveals God's values, His heart, and what He prioritizes as imperative. If God had to choose one primary thing to restore before the Day of the Lord, we might think He would release revival power, or the salvation of nations, or something extraordinary. Indeed, God will restore something close to His heart before the return of Christ - the family unit! Honestly, this reveals to us how significantly God thinks of the role of both the fathers and mothers, as well as the children. Humanity chases after success in all forms, like fame and financial victory, but God looks to our families and the raising up of the next generation as the most valuable in His eyes. As the Body of Christ and as forerunners, it is critical for us to move with God and understand His value system and then align our personal lives and our families to it.

I imagine God looking down the corridors of time to the last generation. The enemy has concentrated on the destruction of our families, marriages and our children as the number one target on his hit list. He relentlessly attacks marriages to break the family unit; he uses the pressure and unrelenting work of the gay agenda in the world, the perversion of pornography, sex-trafficking, and immorality of all sorts accelerated through the internet to leave a trail of destruction behind. I believe there have been cumulative damages that we are beginning to reap as we engage the youth and young adults of this generation. Despite all this brokenness, and there is an unprecedented level, the Lord has not left us alone but promised help to restore the hearts of our children; He has promised us the power and spirit of Elijah to heal and make whole the hearts of both parents and their kids.

THE HEART OF A SHEPHERD

"Then I will give you shepherds after My own heart,
who will feed you on knowledge and understanding.
(Jeremiah 3:15)

This anointing of the spirit and power of Elijah was to turn the hearts of the fathers back to the children, or for a shepherding heart to be cultivated in the older generation to care for and raise up the younger ones. This precisely is what John did as he pastored and shepherded his young disciples. If John was about 30 years old, then most likely his disciples were younger than him, probably teens and young adults. He invested in the next generation to raise up future leaders! This shepherding heart is part and parcel to the forerunner calling. Jeremiah had prophesied that God would send to Israel shepherds after His own heart who will feed the people with knowledge and understanding (Jeremiah 3:15; 23:4). John was one of these shepherds as a foretaste that many more would come in that last generation.

I want to encourage those who are reading this book that age is not a prerequisite to be a shepherd or father/mother in the faith. You don't have to wait until you're older to begin to carry God's shepherd-heart and operate out of it. *More than age and experience, which are valuable, it is the heart posture of caring and investing in people.* Though most of the time the discipling goes downward to those who are younger, I have seen young adults in their early 20's shepherd and counsel men in their 40's and 50's. The point is, don't wait until you are older. Find people to invest your life into. This shepherding heart is one of the most apparent manifestations of the forerunner spirit. Maybe unknown to you, this is how John lived as well. Let us take a closer look at John's life in this regard.

JOHN'S DISCIPLES

Then the disciples of John came to Him…
(Matthew 9:14)

When you think of John the Baptist, what image comes to your mind? Christianity and Hollywood have depicted John as a rogue, lonely prophet, hardly clothed, with a leather belt, living alone in the wilderness eating locusts and honey. He's upset at the religious system and always seems to be in a bad mood preaching fire and brimstone. This image could hardly be closer to the truth.

This may be a surprise to you, but John actually lived in a community. He was not isolated, nor did he run away from the religious community due to authority issues with the Sanhedrin or the Jewish elders. The Bible does not tell us the reason why he grew up in the wilderness; but we know this, he was a rabbi or teacher who had a following of young disciples that he was raising up in the ways of the Lord. John was at most 30 years old when we are introduced to him as he began preaching in the wilderness of Judea. At this point in his life, he already had a group of disciples who were like interns that lived with him, followed him and learned from him. Much like the twelve disciples that were with Jesus, John also had a group of disciples that he invested his life into. If we were to use our modern vernacular, John was part of a local church and would have been running a home group at his house. He was not separated or isolated from the people of God; instead, he was helping train the future leaders.

> *[35]Again the next day John was standing with two of his disciples, [36]and he looked at Jesus as He walked, and said, "Behold, the Lamb of God!" [37]The two disciples heard him speak, and they followed Jesus. (John 1:35-37)*

When John saw Jesus and declared Him to be the Lamb of God, his disciples left him and began following Jesus. John had trained them for this purpose because John knew that his ministry was to decrease so that Jesus' ministry could increase (John 3:30). Of the two disciples that left John this day, one was Andrew, Peter's brother (John 1:40). Andrew not only became one of the twelve original apostles with Christ, but he is the one that also went and introduced Peter to Jesus. John's ministry in the community had prepared at least this disciple to walk with Jesus in his apostolic call. John's heart to raise up young disciples was a manifestation of the spirit and power of Elijah in his life.

THE URGENT NEED FOR FATHERS AND MOTHERS

For if you were to have countless tutors in Christ,
yet you would not have many fathers, for in Christ
Jesus I became your father through the gospel.
(1 Corinthians 4:15)

I have worked closely with youth and young adults at the Sarasota House of Prayer through our staff, Internships, VOICE Ministry and Worship schools, Consecrate conference and the community that has organically formed over these past five years. One thing screams loud and clear to me-- the need for fathers and mothers in the faith to arise and take their position. Let me explain. When we began the house of prayer and even the ministry schools, I thought we needed to find and create the best teaching curriculum. After all, we are a Bible-teaching ministry school. However, I soon realized that putting broken young adults in a prayer room for hours a week and having them attend Bible classes was not enough. I know it sounds blasphemous! Don't stone me yet. We were offering the traditional "prayer and Bible" components, but their hearts were crying out, "Someone help me!" from all the pain of their past. These hungry students were trying their best to seek the Lord and minister to Him, yet their issues would derail them. I found myself talking and counseling more and more and realized that God made us relational beings just as He is. *The truth of the Word and the power of His presence in prayer are best facilitated in a relational discipleship context.* This is exactly what Jesus said when He told us to go and "**make disciples**" in Matthew 28:19. This revelation became a pivotal turning point for me and a passion in my heart!

The brokenness in this generation is staggering and alarming, both inside and outside the Church. We are hitting epidemic levels in our culture. The "good" students who want to serve the Lord are coming in from broken families, fatherless situations, chemical and sexual addictions of all kinds including pornography for both males and females, and the list goes on and on. These young hearts had already faced so much trauma which they were never meant to experience. In attempting to reach this generation, I found that many parents and church groups have loosened the rules thinking they could befriend young people by being culturally relevant. This has only backfired as it allows them to live with their compromised moral compass and doesn't challenge them to grow up. Instead, I believe that at their core young adults are looking for stability, authenticity, and love that sets boundaries. Boundaries communicated in the right way let them know they are for their good. They may not like it at the moment, none of us do, but after the outcome, they can see that we spoke the truth in love for their benefit. Beloved, I'm convinced that young adults are craving for fathers and mothers in the faith who will have the courage to invest their lives into them and love them with compassion and the truth! *The parenting role that many natural and biological fathers and mothers have abdicated, God is sending the spirit of Elijah to raise up spiritual fathers and mothers to nurture and release identity to this hurting generation.*

INVESTING YOUR LIFE

Having so fond an affection for you, we were well-pleased to impart to you not only the gospel of God but also our own lives, because you had become very dear to us. (1 Thessalonians 2:8)

Paul reveals how he discipled and mentored the church in Thessalonica as he planted the congregation and lived among them. It wasn't enough to only teach and share the gospel, but he invested his heart and life into the people. I understand first-hand that spending your life on others is not easy, but this kind of discipleship bears fruit in people's lives. Over the course of our marriage and family life, Jennifer and I have had different seasons of housing and discipling young adults. When we do this, we open our hearts, our house, our kids and the refrigerator to them. They become part of the family for better or for worse, with all of our family's idiosyncrasies, and become one of our "kids." This involves sacrificing of course, but the fruit and joy it bears are far worth it.

Let me share two stories with you. In 2005 I met a young adult named Josh, 21, who sold me a custom computer that he had built. After talking, we found out that he had an extremely broken background and that he needed a place to stay. We had just had our third child, Daniel, and Jennifer made the heroic decision to let Josh move in with us. Josh stayed a year with us, and it was tumultuous with many ups and downs. At one point, for a short time, his older brother and mom were with us as well. His dad moved into our pastor's house, and we were ministering to the entire family! Jennifer, Josh and I would have long conversations as he would go back and forth on different issues of the truth in his heart. At the end of the year, he became offended, left and we did not hear from him for some years. A few years ago, out of the blue, Josh reached out to say hello to us and to thank us for investing in his life. He is now in his 30's and lives in North Carolina, stable with an IT job, part of a local church and doing well.

Another Josh entered into our lives about three years ago. He was 19 years old at the time with a lot of wounds from his past, partially homeless, and going from couch to couch. We got him stabilized immediately at someone's home, and he began to come to the prayer room. Josh would spend hours a day in the Bible as we watched the Lord transform his life. After he completed a six-month internship at IHOPKC, we invited him to move into our house and attend the Voice Ministry School. Over these past two years, we have watched him face head-on the hardest and most painful issues of his past and come out victorious. If you know Josh, he has a loud personality with an incredible gift to preach and influence people. The most rewarding thing for Jennifer and I is watching his heart grow in the Lord and making intentional decisions to mature. He has become a son to us, and we are so glad that we took the plunge to invite him.

I share these stories with you as real-life examples so that you can find your sons and daughters to invest your life into. Over the years Jennifer and I have had the privilege of speaking into so many lives, both individuals and couples, who have come over for dinner, gone out for one-on-one time, or my favorite, tagging along with us while doing errands or working. It takes work and must be intentionally done but investing in people is the way of the Kingdom and the only way to live!

THE COMMITMENT TO DISCIPLESHIP

"Go therefore and make disciples of all the nations, baptizing them in the name of the Father and the Son and the Holy Spirit, (Matthew 28:19)

As you may gather from these pages, nurturing and getting behind young adults so they can soar is a passion for Jennifer and me. We play the "mom and dad" role and watch the Lord bring wholeness into these future leaders. It takes commitment and intentionality on our part, but it can be done. And the most rewarding part is watching the life, character, and fruit of Jesus being instilled in them and come out of them.

We have evolved our entire ministry culture to champion discipling relationships as the context for spiritual growth. At the Sarasota House of Prayer, every one of our staff members and students is being discipled by someone older, sometimes by two different people. They meet one-on-one at least every other week. And the word is spreading so that people in our community at large are now beginning to get involved either discipling or being discipled. The context of discipleship brings stability and an excellent environment for God to heal and equip young (and old) hearts.

If you are a forerunner or you have read this book up to this point, you need to build two strong relationships: the first is with someone you look up to who can spend time with you to father or mother you and disciple you. Preferably this person will be older, but that is not always the case. They should also be your same gender. You can, of course, have more than one of these relationships. Having this consistent input in your life will help you grow steady spiritually, bring stability to your emotions and keep you accountable. Plus, you want someone that will get behind you and cheer you on! For me, the spiritual fathers that I have had in my life have made a significant impact in shaping me, counseling me and giving me the courage to step out when I didn't see myself the way God saw me.

The second relationship I would recommend for your growth is for you to go and find someone to pour your life into. Fulfill the Great Commission by finding someone to invest your strength into and help raise up. It is through the raising up of others that we replicate ourselves and the values the Lord has given us. In this way, we will prepare a generation for the Lord!

KEY UNDERSTANDING

John the Baptist did not live or minister alone. Instead, the archetypical forerunner lived in a community, discipling and teaching the ways of the Lord to his community. This fundamental way of living as a spiritual family with fathers and mothers was always part of the Gospel message. This relational family value is intrinsic to the father-heart of God who is committed to reviving the family unit. End-time forerunners will carry this father-heart of God to build up the next generation and bring healing and restoration to the family of God.

A PRAYER FOR FORERUNNERS

Dear Heavenly Father,

I pray that in our generation You would raise up spiritual fathers and mothers with Your Father-heart to shepherd and form the budding forerunners. Release the Spirit of Elijah to turn the hearts of the fathers and mothers to our broken and wounded children. Give the older generation eyes to see the gold that is in our children and the wisdom to call it out and cultivate their lives. Put a steadfast spirit in them to nurture and invest their hearts and lives into the next generation.

God, I ask for a joining of generations as You build your end-time army. Let there be much healing that is found in these mutually-beneficial discipling relationships. Build the family of God once again to show forth the glory of the Father's divine love and wisdom. Equip and mobilize the family of God in our generation to fulfill the Great Commission of making disciples of all nations.

Raise up forerunners whose lives are genuine inside and out and who are committed to healthy relationships, marriages, and families. Let these forerunners carry both the forerunner message but also the heart of God that fuels this message. May the testimony of their lives be a clear witness to the goodness of God's love and mercy.

In Jesus' glorious Name,

Amen!

CHAPTER 10

MORE THAN A PROPHET

The Joy of Being a Friend of the Bridegroom

ONE LAST REQUEST

²Now when John, while imprisoned, heard of the works of Christ, he sent word by his disciples ³and said to Him, "Are You the Expected One, or shall we look for someone else?" (Matthew 11:2-3)

John's life had been marked by the supernatural power of God. As he sat in the prison cell alone with little-to-no hope of getting out, I'm sure he began to ponder if he had done the right thing in confronting Herod's sin. He had boldly and methodically called out Herod's adultery, and now he was paying the price. John had prepared for so long in the wilderness, almost thirty years. He was just about six months into his preaching and baptizing ministry when the king imprisoned him. It seemed that at the height of his popularity everything came to a halt. Then he spent almost two years in prison-- doubts and thoughts surely began to swirl in his head. "If only he had been quiet before Herod, he could still have ministered to the rest of Israel..." The prototypical forerunner who was announced by the angel Gabriel at his conception, prophesied over by his father at birth, trained in the wilderness of Judea, and was thrust into a preaching ministry by the word of the Lord was now sitting in a dark cell day after day. The worst part was, he didn't even get to see his cousin, Jesus, minister. He had only heard of the works of Christ from afar in his prison cell.

John had served the call of God on his life. He had prepared the people of Israel to receive the Lamb of God, and when the Messiah had come, John willingly gave up his ministry so as not to rival his cousin. He said, "***Jesus must increase, and I must decrease***" (John 3:30). John understood that the context of his ministry was a preparatory work for the people of Israel. The initiative to decrease revealed John's humility and showed that he ministered for the sake of Christ, not himself. He was willing to lay down his calling so the focus and attention would be on the ministry of Jesus from then on.

As a side note about personal callings: I believe it's important to understand what God has called us to personally and how He has gifted us. However, so many young and old seem to chase after the fulfillment of what they think their individual calling is and how it should look. Our gifts and callings may be powerful and relevant; however, I have witnessed the freedom found in submitting our individual gifts and callings to serve the higher call of Jesus in our generation. Remember, Jesus is the One who gave us our gifts and callings. If we submit to God's dream, then the focus becomes about Christ and His Kingdom and less about ourselves and our role. This shift in focus relieves pressure, allows us to serve with joy, and uses our skills to further the work of God in our generation. British Bible teacher Arthur Wallis said it best, "Find out what God is doing in your generation and throw yourself wholly into it."

John gathered his disciples, those who were still with him, and sent them to Jesus to ask Him one last question, *"Was He the Expected One or should we look for another?"* (Matthew 11:3). Meaning did John make a mistake in confronting Herod or did he make the right choice in paying the price to lay down his life for the Messiah to come. John knew he had made the right choice, but the longer he waited in prison, the more the doubts began to come. Finally, he had to find out one last time. Even the great forerunner needed reassurance for his faith.

4Jesus answered and said to them, "Go and report to John what you hear and see: 5the blind receive sight and the lame walk, the lepers are cleansed, and the deaf hear, the dead are raised up, and the poor have the gospel preached to them. (Matthew 11:4-5)

Jesus answered John by quoting two famous Old Testament promises of what the Messiah would do when he came-- Isaiah 35:5 and Isaiah 61:1. John himself, who was identified by Isaiah 40, would have understood what these two messianic passages meant. Jesus was saying that the Messiah was here and that He was the long-awaited King of Israel. In essence, Jesus was reassuring John that he had made the right choice to sacrifice for Him. This reply was just what John needed. Yet at the end of His statement, Jesus adds one more peculiar comment about not being offended.

TEMPTATION TO BE OFFENDED

"And blessed is he who does not take offense at Me."
(Matthew 11:6)

To start, this is an odd comment that Jesus makes. He is obviously addressing John and answering the question that John's disciples posed to him. However, at the end of his answer, Jesus tells John that there is a blessing to those who are not offended at Him. What is Jesus saying and why is He bringing this up? I believe John was at a crossroads at the end of his life and Jesus was drawing out the war of affections that was happening in John's heart. Jesus wanted John to finish well. This prison cell was John's last hurdle after a life well spent, and Jesus was going to help him overcome.

Beloved, if you haven't found out by now, you will soon: All those that choose to follow Jesus will be tempted to become offended and leave Him at some point. He is the *"stone of stumbling and a rock of offense"* (1 Peter 2:8) to the carnal way of life-- thinking and desires which unfortunately are ingrained in all of us. *When a genuine pursuit of God is birthed in our hearts, our biggest obstacle is not the enemy, its actually facing and overcoming our own brokenness, carnality, and selfishness.* Jesus, the Rock, becomes the unmovable truth in love that every hungry pursuer of God must face. And when we find Him, we come to a fork in the road. Either we submit and follow on the road to freedom from ourselves, or we become offended and create our own way. The first temptation is to take up offense! Mike Bickle, the director of the International House of Prayer in Kansas City, says it best, "God offends the mind to reveal the heart." *I believe every genuine believer will face this temptation to be offended at Jesus on multiple occasions in their lives because He doesn't do things the way that we think He should or when He should!* Truly His ways are not our ways (Isaiah 55:8-9).

John ran into this fork in the road of his life, and the persuasion to be offended by Jesus challenged him to the core. Sitting in a prison cell for close to two years will help do that to you! The snare for offense arises when Jesus does not meet or outright goes against the unsaid expectations in our hearts. Sometimes, probably most times, we don't even know these expectations are there. I don't believe that John ever thought his life would end up this way. His ministry exploded out of the gate, holding large conferences in the desert. Then, suddenly, he was imprisoned and seemingly set aside by God. How did John respond? How would you respond if you found yourself in that same situation?

"He who has the bride is the bridegroom; but the friend of the bridegroom, who stands and hears him, rejoices greatly because of the bridegroom's voice. So this joy of mine has been made full. (John 3:29)

After the storm of doubts and emotions subsided in John, I believe he rejoiced in the bridegroom. Even beyond being the messenger and voice of preparation, his highest identity was standing before Jesus as His friend. John calls himself "the friend of the bridegroom" and his joy was connected to the joy of his friend. This identification shows how intricately linked his life and heart were to the bridegroom. Jesus validates John as He begins to evaluate his life, and He uses it as a lesson for His generation.

CONDEMNATION OF HIS GENERATION

[7]As these men were going away, Jesus began to speak to the crowds about John, "What did you go out into the wilderness to see? A reed shaken by the wind? [8]"But what did you go out to see? A man dressed in soft clothing? Those who wear soft clothing are in kings' palaces! [9]"But what did you go out to see? A prophet? Yes, I tell you, and one who is more than a prophet. (Matthew 11:7-9)

Jesus then turns to the crowd of people who had gathered around Him and began to evaluate John's ministry. He asks them three separate times, "What did you go out into the wilderness to see?" (Matthew 11:7-9). We have to understand the context to appreciate what Jesus is asking. Remember, John was preaching in the wilderness of Judea; to hear him or visit his ministry, it had to be an intentional effort. The crowd Jesus was addressing were the ones who had taken the time to make the journey out into the wilderness. They weren't the casual Christians, if we can use that term; rather, this was the committed group who wanted to check out the latest phenomenon and be near the cutting edge of what God is doing. "What did they go out to see?"

> *[16]"But to what shall I compare this generation? It is like children sitting in the marketplaces, who call out to the other children, [17]and say, 'We played the flute for you, and you did not dance; we sang a dirge, and you did not mourn.' [18]"For John came neither eating nor drinking, and they say, 'He has a demon!' [19]"The Son of Man came eating and drinking, and they say, 'Behold, a gluttonous man and a drunkard, a friend of tax collectors and sinners!' Yet wisdom is vindicated by her deeds." (Matthew 11:16-19)*

Before commenting on John's ministry, let me carry out the train of thought that Jesus had as he began to challenge His generation in verses 16-19. He takes the question about John and extrapolates it to comment on the people of Israel. Jesus compares the Jews of His age to a group of children sitting in the marketplace who are not moved to action or change by the messengers that God has sent. He reveals that God sent John to warn Israel by singing the dirge of lament over their sins, but the people didn't respond. Instead, they said that John had a demon! They said that his lifestyle of fasting and praying and his message of repentance was too radical. They didn't heed his warning to change; surprisingly, they accused him of being demon-possessed!

Then the Father sent Jesus who came from the opposite direction of John, eating and drinking, or "playing the flute;" yet they did not dance. They did not respond to the message that Jesus brought. The same group who accused John also denied Jesus, calling him a "*gluttonous man and a drunkard, a friend of tax collectors and sinners*" (Matthew 11:19). Jesus' question to them was "what did you go out to see in John?" because they didn't react or change. Jesus might have wondered, "Why did you spend the energy in time and money to go visit John in the wilderness when you chose not to listen to him, but instead hurled stones of accusation against him?" God was condemning that generation because they did not respond to the visitation or invitation that He sent. Where does our generation stand? Have we heard and reacted to the message that our spiritual fathers have brought in this past generation?

JESUS VALIDATES JOHN'S MINISTRY

⁹"But what did you go out to see? A prophet? Yes, I tell you, and one who is more than a prophet. ¹⁰"This is the one about whom it is written, 'Behold, I send My messenger ahead of you, who will prepare your way before you.' (Matthew 11:9-11)

Set between Jesus asking the crowd and then condemning and rebuking His generation for not responding to the message that He and John brought is His assessment of John's life and ministry. He baited them in asking, "Did you go out to see John who was a prophet?" because He knew how reverently Israel held the prophets of old. *Jesus declares over John that he was indeed a prophet but more than a prophet.* Yes, God raised up John to be a voice from Heaven, but Jesus was saying there is something greater than being used by God prophetically. John was the forerunner, or God's divine "messenger," who was sent to prepare the people of God.

In the charismatic clamor of our day where so many people want to be "prophetic" or are looking to be a prophet or an apostle, where these callings or positions are almost idolized, Jesus assessment of John gives us some clear perspective. I believe Jesus' affirmation of John's ministry is two-fold and summed up in his identity that he was "More than a Prophet."

MORE THAN A PROPHET

For I am jealous for you with a godly jealousy; for I betrothed you to one husband so that to Christ I might present you as a pure virgin.
(2 Corinthians 11:2)

The quality that made John more than a prophet as the forerunner messenger of God was his heart to prepare the people of God and present them to Jesus. I believe we as forerunner messengers must operate from the identity of being a friend of the bridegroom. We deliver the message with the heart of God for the joy of the bridegroom's inheritance. Jesus once again affirms this forerunner aspect that was prophesied over John at his birth. John's primary role as a messenger was not just to expose sin through his preaching but to have the heart of the people prepared through the baptism of repentance so that they could receive Messiah. It is walking in this identity, a friend of the bridegroom, which is so unique and dear to the heart of God.

In the Jewish culture, the friend of the bridegroom helped the groom by making the prior arrangements for his marriage. One or two friends would assist the bride, bringing her to the bridegroom before the consummation. Afterward, they were able to certify to the wedding guests that the fulfillment of the marriage had taken place and the joyous festivities could continue. John gladly took on this role as the friend of the bridegroom! John expressed his genuine joy that the people were accepting Jesus. John's gladness and priority were wrapped up and found in Jesus' desire and will. When Jesus fulfilled His purpose, John not only celebrated it, but the Bible says that his "joy was made full."

Paul, the apostle, also carried this same type of spirit for the Body of Christ. He was jealous over the infants in Christ with godly jealousy to protect and prepare them so that he could present them to Jesus as pure. I believe that God is raising up end-time forerunners who will not separate themselves but love the Body of Christ, protecting and preparing them for the transitions that are coming unto the return of Christ.

In the same way, the Lord is raising up forerunners to challenge and confront the sleeping giant in the western nations-- the slumbering Church. The Lord will use forerunners to awaken the Church, though it will not be easy nor pretty. It will more likely be uncomfortable, challenging, painful and offensive for those who think of themselves as good Christians who attend "Church" but are living with a dull, entertainment spirit. *This exposing will happen by our lifestyles as much as our message.* God is jealous for the full affection and devotion of His Bride and will send these anointed messengers to challenge the status quo in our generation.

Forerunners, are you ready for this type of confrontation in love?

It will be costly like it was for John, but it is part of God's plan to awaken the Church. This is why you are called! Take courage and go deep in God's Word and heart. Be bold in humility and commit to a righteous lifestyle that will effuse the fragrance of Christ wherever you go.

KEY UNDERSTANDING

Jesus validated John's life and ministry as being more than a local preacher who spoke the truth to His people. Jesus called him *More Than a Prophet* - namely the greatest man ever born! Jesus also states that *"the one who is least in the kingdom of heaven is greater than John"* (Matthew 11:11). In this comparison to all those that follow after John in the New Covenant, there is an open invitation to greatness, meaning experiencing God through the Holy Spirit. Traditionally, this has been understood to contrast believers who have the privileges of the New Covenant dispensation, like the indwelling Holy Spirit, to those believers who, like John, were part of the Old Covenant. While this is true, I believe we can take part in this open invitation through the Holy Spirit, who brings us further into this paradigm of being a Friend of the Bridegroom. This friendship includes the glory and intimacy of experiencing God's emotions as well as knowing His thoughts, including the plan of redemption so that we can partner with Him in it. John was the herald of Jesus' first coming, but I don't think he understood the end-time events as we do since we have the fully unveiled Scriptures.

Beloved forerunners, we have an immense privilege and opportunity to walk and live as friends of the Bridegroom and to partner with Jesus in preparing His global End-Time Bride for Himself! In this, our generation can stand with the shepherd heart of God and enter in as More Than Prophets in serving the Body of Christ.

Thank you dear forerunner, for your courage to say "yes" to God and to stand with Him when things don't make sense to your mind. Thank you for plowing the ground into new territory, embracing truth, sacrificing your desires and pressing forward against the culture's tide. My conviction is that the raising up of forerunners, like yourself, in this hour is God's mercy for the Church and His primary strategy to make Jesus known. I can't wait to hear all the heroic hidden forerunner God stories when we meet on that sea of crystal glass!

A FATHER'S BLESSING

Dear forerunner,

*I bless the courageous flame that burns within your soul; the fire that drives you for more. Don't let it **ever** go out.*

I bless your resolve in hope against hope that you would continue to believe for change and the fullness of God's dream for your generation, and that you will not settle for less during the difficulties of your journey.

I bless your heart with humility and a teachable spirit so that you receive God's training and shaping of your heart even when you don't understand His ways.

I bless your steadfast and immovable spirit from the Word of God as the foundational compass for your life.

I bless your identity as a friend of the bridegroom-- to serve and prepare the people of God for the bridegroom's sake.

May God's richest blessing be upon you in Jesus' Name!

AMEN!

ABOUT THE AUTHOR

Roger and Jennifer Lee have a burden to see the Lord renew a culture of prayer within His Church, and to see God's intervention in this present generation. They both carry a shepherd's heart and a clear message of consecration and holiness unto the Lord.

Roger and Jennifer have been married since 2001 and have ten beautiful sons and daughters! Together they serve as the executive directors of the Sarasota House of Prayer missions base and oversee the training center.

The Sarasota House of Prayer missions base is committed to the Great Commission and proclaiming Christ's return by establishing night and day prayer, discipling and equipping believers, and declaring the Gospel to the lost.

Central to the Sarasota House of Prayer is the Prayer Room, a sanctuary set apart to grow in your relationship with Jesus. Intercession and devotional times, led by various worship teams from throughout the region, draws the presence of God into our region. Changing the spiritual atmosphere minimizes what the enemy can do in our region as well as enhance and multiply the efforts of what the Church and parachurch ministries are doing already.

For more information visit our website:

sarasotahop.com

Sarasota House of Prayer Missions Base, 1872 18th St., Sarasota, FL 34234
www.sarasotahop.com

MINISTRY AND WORSHIP SCHOOL

VOICE MINISTRY SCHOOL

The vision for the **VOICE Ministry School** (VMS) is to raise up leaders whose voice and lifestyle will penetrate the culture and bring reformation to their generation.

2 TRACKS

Discipleship Intensive: Accelerated Leadership - 9 months

Ministry Training: Comprehensive School - 2 years

VMS is a hybrid school combining Personal Discipleship with Bible School training. Students come to encounter God and learn their identity in the context of day and night prayer. We strive to develop a biblical value system and theological basis for Christian maturity, ethics and service as they experience transformation in the Word of God through the power of the Holy Spirit.

For more information visit our website:

sarasotahop.com

Sarasota House of Prayer Missions Base, 1872 18th St., Sarasota, FL 34234
www.sarasotahop.com

MINISTRY AND WORSHIP SCHOOL

VOICE WORSHIP SCHOOL

The vision of the **VOICE Worship School** (VWS) is to deepen the expression of worship throughout our region by training and equipping worship leaders and musicians.

VWS combines biblical theology with a heart of devotion and musical excellence that ushers others into the presence of God through worship. Singers, musicians and worship leaders are equipped and trained to confidently minister to the Lord, and to communicate the power of the gospel through music and song.

For more information visit our website:

sarasotahop.com

Sarasota House of Prayer Missions Base, 1872 18th St., Sarasota, FL 34234
www.sarasotahop.com

JUNIOR WORSHIP SCHOOL

The vision of the Junior Worship School (ages 8-15) is to engage younger children with the love of music and to train and equip them in worship.

The Junior Worship School offers professional, age-specific training for young worshippers. Students will receive classical instruction in a contemporary worship environment.

For more information visit our website:
sarasotahop.com

Sarasota House of Prayer Missions Base, 1872 18th St., Sarasota, FL 34234
www.sarasotahop.com

MAPS GLOBAL

MISSIONS AND PRAYER SCHOOL

The Sarasota House of Prayer is partnering with MAPS Global to launch a satellite location for the Missions and Prayer School!

MAPS is a one-year experience in prayer and missions with 1 semester of training and 1 semester of frontier missions.

MAPS Global is a frontier missions organization focused on mobilizing, training and sending singing missionaries to plant and build bases for prayer, worship, outreach, and training in strategic cities across the 10/40 window. We believe that God is stirring a STUDENT AWAKENING in America unto another STUDENT VOLUNTEER movement to the ends of the earth! Be a part of finishing the Great Commission in our generation.

For more information visit our website:

sarasotahop.com or mapsglobal.org

Sarasota House of Prayer Missions Base, 1872 18th St., Sarasota, FL 34234
www.sarasotahop.com

i   n   t   e   r   s   h   i   p

A part-time internship raising up wholehearted messengers who know and proclaim the gospel. (RE)new Internship will equip you to have a Biblical Worldview and to know the Biblical Gospel message.

Unfortunately, many secular worldviews have seeped into the Church and have mixed with Christianity resulting in many devastating impacts to our faith. In this internship, we break down these false worldviews and build up a Biblical Worldview. The goal of the internship is to renew our minds with the truth of the Scriptures so that we are equipped to walk out our faith rightly for the rest of our days and so that we can articulate these truths to others.

Our internships exist to equip believers in the Word of God, that they might minister in the power of the Holy Spirit, engage in intercession, and be committed to outreach and service. Our vision is to work in relationship with the larger Body of Christ to engage in the Great Commission, as we seek to walk out the two great commandments to love God and people.

For more information visit our website:

sarasotahop.com

Sarasota House of Prayer Missions Base, 1872 18th St., Sarasota, FL 34234
www.sarasotahop.com

95958091R00111

Made in the USA
Columbia, SC
27 May 2018